It is my pleasure to recommend to you the book, "Fueling the Nazarene Movement with Love." My friend, Larry McKain, and a great team of leaders have presented the missional account of the Church of the Nazarene as an amazing multiplying agent for Jesus in the world. It is encouraging, inspiring, relevant and well presented. This book and these leaders are a gift to the Master's church!

Rev. Mark J Bane
Director of Evangelism and New Church Development
USA/Canada Region Church of the Nazarene

Practical, relevant, and purposeful describe the wealth of wisdom and experience awaiting the reader of "Fueling the Nazarene Movement with Love." Written with a desire for a passionate renewal of the church's commission to make disciples, this book will challenge your heart and provide inspirational and intentional ideas to help you serve your community with grace and truth. Thanks to my friend, Dr. Larry McKain, a visionary leader who loves the church and has championed this project to equip us for a future fueled by faith!

Dr. Keith Newman, President
Southern Nazarene University

This book is a work of a group of people who love the growth of the Kingdom of God. We waited a long time for this project to be finished. God has planted us in a missionary church and we believe that this contribution will greatly help us to do the work of making Christlike disciples in the nations. I applaud this project, its leadership and their passion for church growth and multiplication.

Dr. Elias Betanzos, Lead Pastor
Center of Praise and Proclamation – Oaxaca, Mexico
President of the Mexico Board – Church of the Nazarene

Two decades ago Larry McKain saw a need few others saw and went to work crafting a solution nobody asked him for. The result was a system for training and coaching church planters that over the next 8 years would impact 5,400 leaders in 25 denominations. Several USA districts have something in common: large, multiplying churche̶ ̶ ̶ ̶ ̶ ̶ trained and coached by Larry. Now he is at it again, h̶ ̶ ̶ ̶ ̶ ̶ ̶ ̶ ̶ ̶ ̶ ̶ ̶ body sees and having spent hundreds of hours ̶ ̶ ̶ ̶ ̶ ̶ ̶ ̶ ̶ ̶ ̶ him for. I expect that 20 years from now, t̶l̶ ̶ ̶ ̶ ̶ ̶ ̶ ̶ ̶ r themselves.

̶ott Sherwood
Superintendent

D1295068

"Fueling the Nazarene Movement with Love" is the work that our denomination has been waiting for! Don't just read it, apply it and watch the Holy Spirit move in your local congregation!

Dr. Adam Lewis, Lead Pastor
Decatur First Church – Decatur, Illinois

The **MULTIPLYNAZ** *series is a treasure! It gathers the wisdom, insight, and passion of great disciple-makers and Kingdom-leaders into a delightful mash-up that catalyzes and resources the church at every level. Wherever* **MULTIPLYNAZ** *is used, conversations and cultures will be shaped toward greater Kingdom impact.*

Rev. Kyle Poole
Georgia District Superintendent

"Fueling the Nazarene Movement, Book One," is a refreshing and optimistic paradigm of the Church of the Nazarene. It reminds us of the great commission of the church in the midst of cultural drift. The mission is inspired with vision and hope to reach lost and broken people with the transforming message of Jesus. The practical insights will help to guide a multiplication movement for church planting.*

Dr. Kevin C. Donley
Wisconsin District Superintendent

A desire for a Multiplication Movement is born out of love for God, love for others, and love for the church. No one loves the church, and the vibrant possibilities of the church more than Dr. Larry McKain. In the first book of the **MULTIPLYNAZ** *series he powerfully and beautifully has worked with a team of leaders to describe what loving the church, and thus, a loving church looks like. I highly recommend the book to all who want the church to be a light in darkness.*

Dr. Greg Mason
North Carolina District Superintendent

A must read for every pastor and layperson. This book emphasizes the movement of God through Nazarenes and our need to revisit our roots as we anticipate the future.

Dr. Mark Berry
Alabama South District Superintendent

I highly recommend to you the book "Fueling the Nazarene Movement with Love." I found it both compelling and practical. The ideas and stories will inspire the reader to make a difference where you serve presently. It will resonate with anyone who has a passion to make Christlike disciples in our world.

Dr. Ron Blake
Indianapolis District Superintendent

"Agenda Harmony" is important to any organization or movement that desires to make a significant impact. Sometimes this occurs without intentional thought but as an organization grows in complexity it often requires focused analysis as to aspired- to outcomes and "ways of doing." You will find this book provides information that leads to unity of purpose and practice.

Dr. Jim Cooper
Southwest Oklahoma District Superintendent

This book and the **MULTIPLYNAZ** *series come to the church at a time when we need this message. With great temptations to be pulled in different directions, this book will help us understand ourselves, the mission we are on and will help keep the church focused on evangelism, church planting and spiritual health. I strongly commend it.*

Dr. Keith Wright
Retired District Superintendent Mentor

The time is now, or as Dr. Bill Sullivan wrote, "twenty years ago" to plant a church or ministry. "Fueling the Nazarene Movement with Love" is a great and timely piece of work for church leaders, laymen and clergy alike. There is no better time for the church to be the church than today! The world we live in is desperate need of the truth. The truth is within us, the church. By the grace of God we have all been called to a great and higher calling, and that is, to empower the church.

Rev. Greg Garman
Los Angeles District Superintendent

The **MULTIPLYNAZ** *series will be a guide to help all of us on our journey of making Christlike disciples.*

Rev. Phil Rhoades
Joplin District Superintendent

This book would have been such a welcome resource when I began the journey of being a District Superintendent. I am glad it is available going forward. Thanks to all who have worked to make this tool a reality!

Dr. Bob Mahaffey
Southwest Ohio District Superintendent

"Fueling the Nazarene Movement" helps to remind us that we are a connected church with a collective mission to join God in His redemptive work throughout the world. May God be glorified and His church edified through the collaborative efforts of this book.

Rev. Lynnlee Moser, Director of NexGen / The Collective
USA/Canada Region

Clarity and alignment are two ingredients needed to achieve traction with mission and vision fulfilment. Our prayer is that this work will guide our church to fruitful expansion as we achieve the call of Jesus, "to make Christlike disciples in the nations."

Rev. Wynne Lankford, Lead Pastor
Southside Church – Richmond, Virginia

I would like to thank my colleague, Dr. Larry McKain, for his work with this team and his insightful approach to church health and expansion found in the **MULTIPLYNAZ** *series. I am very grateful for everyone's faithfulness and diligence in bringing this project to pass.*

Dr. David Downs
West Texas District Superintendent

I truly believe this book series is going to usher in a cultural change in our denomination resulting in even more churches multiplying! It truly does reveal the what, why, and how of the fresh wind of fire being ignited across the globe in the Church of the Nazarene! I hope every Nazarene reads every book in this series.

Rev. Ron Riddle, Lead Pastor
Crossroads Cowboy Church – El Paso, Arkansas

"Fueling the Nazarene Movement with Love" is an outstanding book describing 'who' the Nazarenes we are. It is the tool needed to carry the Nazarene message, and a great resource for the training of leaders.

Rev. Caleb Herrera
Texas-Oklahoma Latin American District Superintendent

"Fueling the Nazarene Movement with Love" helps us understand the need to look at the church with new eyes. Actually, it is a call to reclaim Jesus' original intention for the church. This book helps us think, act, and collaborate in ways that fuel the movement of God among the people of God. We need courageous leaders and churches that know how to connect with the least, the last and the lost in the same way that Jesus did, resulting in transformed lives, families, and communities. This book will help us do so.

Rev. Steve Hoffman
Prairie Lakes District Superintendent

In an era of programs, we have sometimes forgotten that what the world needs is the love of Jesus. This book captures the vision of how we, as Christ followers, can reclaim the mantel of leading with love. Let's read and then lead with the love of Jesus.

Rev. Jay Height, Pastor & Inner-City Consultant
Shepherd Community Church – Indianapolis, Indiana

This project will shape the church, her pastors, and her laypersons to be more effective for the Kingdom. I believe we are on the cusp of an amazing breakthrough in the church and this will help turn that tide. A big thank you goes to everyone for the time, effort, and stewardship that has been invested to make the **MULTIPLYNAZ** *project possible. I plan to implement this tool everywhere I have influence.*

Rev. Douglas S. Wyatt
Eastern Kentucky District Superintendent

There have been few works in our movement that have captured the essence of our identity while also preparing us for our future. This is one of those books! I believe that God will use this work to fuel the next great movement in the Church of the Nazarene.

Rev. Wendell Brown
North Central Ohio District Superintendent

MULTIPLYNAZ *is a new Nazarene tool to assist churches and districts who have a passion to multiply believers, disciples, and congregations. Over 35 years of ministry, I have watched Dr. Larry McKain live a life committed to loving the church and resourcing healthy, multiplying churches throughout the world. This book series flows from his heart to help fuel the Nazarene movement by building agenda harmony within districts. I pray every Nazarene who loves God and loves their neighbor will read this book and give themselves fully to the mission of multiplying Christlike disciples in the nations!*

Dr. Jerry Porter
General Superintendent Emeritus
Church of the Nazarene

If you're a leader in the Church of the Nazarene, the **MULTIPLYNAZ** *series is exactly what you've been waiting for. The first book, "Fueling the Nazarene Movement with Love," serves as a foundation for renewing the mission of making disciples and multiplying churches. Dr. Larry McKain has given his life to coaching church planters, pastors, and leaders. Through this project, he continues to do what he does best—fan the flames of the Nazarene Multiplication Movement. I highly recommend not only reading this book, but applying the principles outlined in these pages.*

Dr. Brian L. Powell
Kentucky District Superintendent

"We hear the sounds of a new movement coming." These are hopeful words as we dream about leading others into a relationship with Jesus. The authors have a heart to move us away from just doing church to sparking a multiplying movement of Christ followers that would do whatever it takes to see people come to know Jesus personally. May the words of this book breathe life into us and push us outside our comfort zones in the ways we think about and "do church."

Rev. Kevin Donoho
Crossbridge Community Church
Ottawa, Illinois

When leaders come together caring, sharing with one another and building agenda harmony, awesome results can be anticipated. That's one reason I am humbled and grateful to be a tiny part of this tremendous project. May this resource fuel our faith and prove effective in reaching many new souls through our people, our churches, our districts and beyond.

Rev. Kerry Willis
Philadelphia District Superintendent

Are you looking for a roadmap, a guide, to Kingdom expansion? The **MULTIPLYNAZ** *series offers a fresh approach to the Church of the Nazarene. Larry McKain has coached, trained, and inspired many leaders over many years to expand the church by multiplication. Now, he and a great many other contributors have developed some amazing resources for Pastors, Superintendents, Church Planters, and laity that will help fuel a new movement in the Church of the Nazarene. This series will inspire you to think and act differently for Kingdom expansion.*

Rev. Kevin Hardy
Michigan District Superintendent

This book not only identifies the key ingredients for creating a contagious church — desire, resources and climate—but also demonstrates how such ingredients must work in a Trinitarian kind of way to build such culture. I believe Larry's challenge to rethink our church planting constructs (including Large Launch church planting) and the mobilization of our college students must be taken seriously if we are going fuel the Nazarene movement forward.

Rev. Dave Anderson
Oregon Pacific District Superintendent

I was blessed to have Dr. Larry McKain as a coach when I was a brand new pastor of a brand new church. He was a constant source of encouragement to me and shared his passion to start new churches that reach new people with the love of Jesus. This book brings us hope that truly, in our tribe, the best is yet to come!

Rev. Brett Rickey, Lead Pastor
Highland Park Church
Lakeland, Florida

CHURCH OF THE NAZARENE
MULTIPLYNAZ

Fueling the Nazarene Movement with Love

With 60+ Nazarene Leaders Participating from Across the Church

The **MULTIPLYNAZ** Series—Book One

Fueling the Nazarene Movement with Love
The **MULTIPLYNAZ** Series—Book One

Copyright © 2020 by **MULTIPLYNAZ**
    First Draft Printing, February 2020

Requests for information should be addressed to:
    The **MULTIPLYNAZ** Office
    70 Castle Coombe Ct.
    Bourbonnais, IL 60914

MULTIPLYNAZ Mission: "To resource healthy, multiplying Nazarene churches & districts"

Additional copies may be ordered online at www.multipynaz.org or by calling 913-574-7565.

ISBN: 978-0-578-63781-5

All scripture quotations, unless otherwise indicated, are taken from the Holy Bible: New International Version. NIV. Copyright © 1973, 1978, 1984, 2011 by Biblica, Inc. Used by permission of Zondervan. All rights reserved worldwide.

Scripture quotations marked Msg are from The Message. Copyright © 1993, 1994, 1995, 1996, 2000, 2001, 2002. Used by permission of NavPress Publishing Group.

All rights reserved. No part of this publication may be reproduced, stored in a retrieval system, or transmitted in any form or by any means—electronic; mechanical, photocopy, recording, or any other— except for brief quotations in printed reviews, without the prior permission of the publisher.

Interior layout and cover design by Leanna Brunner
Final editing by Denise McKain

Spanish translation by SINERGIA, an editorial collaborative ministry directed by Juan R. Vázquez Pla, info@synergymediaservices.com.

Printed in the United States of America

We first of all dedicate this book series to the new believers who are among us. The church exists for you. We anticipate there will be over two million of you in the coming few years, many from global cities! We welcome you to a global movement of God through the people of God. Thanks for accepting our invitation to get to know us better. You belong among us. You will find warm fellowship, rich diversity, compassionate hearts, a global mission and a desire to be Christlike that guides everything we do.

We also dedicate this book series to the unsung, front-line heroes of our districts: lay leaders, church planters, pastors of churches large and small who have served the church in the past and present, visionary professors, passionate university students who see the world, not just as it is but as it can be, a movement of leaders who unselfishly give themselves week by week for the vision of Christ's church. God knows each of you by name (Exodus 33:17) and "He will not forget your work and the love you have shown Him as you have helped His people and continue to help them" (Hebrews 6:10).

We finally dedicate this book series to the growing team of multiplying leaders on 480+ Nazarene districts throughout the world who are joining this movement of God through the people of God to create a future we as Nazarenes all dream about and already see happening among us. We are on a wonderful journey together. As John Wesley said, "The best of all is, God is with us!"

Contents

Rev. Terry Armstrong   Terry serves as Superintendent of the Illinois District (Central USA Field) on the USA/Canada Region.

Dr. Virgil Askren   Virgil serves as Superintendent of the South Arkansas District (South Central USA Field) on the USA/Canada Region.

Rev. Mark Bane   Mark serves as the Director of Evangelism and New Church Development for the USA/Canada Region.

Rev. David Bartley   David serves as Superintendent of the North-west Indiana District (Central USA Field) on the USA/Canada Region.

Rev. Dave Bennett   Dave serves as Lead Pastor of Fairview Village Church, located in the suburbs of Philadelphia, Pennsylvania.

Dr. Mark Berry   Mark serves as Superintendent of the Alabama South District (Southeast USA Field) on the USA/Canada Region.

Dr. Elias Betanzos   Elias serves as Superintendent of the Norponiente Oaxaca District (South Mexico Field) and Pastor of the Center of Prayer and Proclamation, the largest Nazarene church in North America.

Dr. Ron Blake   Ron serves as Superintendent of the Indianapolis District (Central USA Field) on the USA/Canada Region.

Rev. Rose Brower-Young   Rose serves as Superintendent of the Canada West District (Canada Field) on the USA/Canada Region.

Rev. Wendell Brown   Wendell serves as Superintendent of the North
                       Central Ohio District (East Central USA Field)
                       on the USA/Canada Region.

Dr. Jim Cooper   Jim serves as Superintendent of the Southwest
                       Oklahoma District (South Central USA Field)
                       on the USA/Canada Region.

Rev. Tim Crump   Tim serves as Superintendent of the Southwest
                       Indiana District (Central USA Field) on the
                       USA/Canada Region.

Dr. Kevin Donley   Kevin serves as Superintendent of the
                       Wisconsin District (Central USA Field) on the
                       USA/Canada Region.

Dr. David Downs   David serves as Superintendent of the West
                       Texas District (South Central USA Field) on the
                       USA/Canada Region.

Dr. Ian Fitzpatrick   Ian serves as the National Director of the Church
                       of the Nazarene in Canada as well as the Super-
                       intendent of the Canada Quebec District
                       (Canada Field) on the USA/Canada Region.

Rev. Sam Flores   Sam serves as Superintendent of the South
                       Carolina District (Southeast USA Field) on the
                       USA/Canada Region.

Rev. Chuck Fountain   Chuck serves as Superintendent of the
                       Louisiana District (South Central USA Field)
                       on the USA/Canada Region.

Dr. Wenton Fyne   Wenton serves as the Senior Pastor of
                       Brooklyn Beulah Nazarene Church located
                       in Brooklyn, New York.

Rev. Greg Garman	Greg serves as Superintendent of the Los Angeles District (Southwest USA Field) on the USA/Canada Region.
Rev. Dan Gilmore	Dan serves as Superintendent of the Northern Michigan District (Central USA Field) on the USA/Canada Region.
Dr. Dwight Gunter	Dwight serves as Superintendent of the Mid-South District (Southeast USA Field) on the USA/Canada Region.
Rev. Kevin Hardy	Kevin serves as Superintendent of the Michigan District (Central USA Field) on the USA/ Canada Region.
Rev. Paul Hartley	Paul serves as Superintendent of the Alaska District (Northwest USA Field) on the USA/ Canada Region.
Rev. Jon & Teri Hauser	Jon and Teri Hauser are co-founders of Prairie Heights Community Church in Fargo, North Dakota and are now involved in a ministry of church development coaching.
Rev. Jay Height	Jay serves as Executive Director of Shepherd Community Center in Indianapolis, Indiana and is a Nazarene Compassionate Ministries USA/ Canada consultant.
Rev. Caleb Herrera	Caleb serves as Superintendent of the Texas/ Oklahoma Latin American District (South Central USA Field) on the USA/Canada Region.
Rev. Steve Hoffman	Steve serves as Superintendent of the Prairie Lakes District (North Central USA Field) on the USA/Canada Region.

Rev. Albert Hung | Albert serves as Superintendent of the Northern California District (Southwest USA Field) on the USA/Canada Region.

Rev. Christine Hung | Christine serves as Director of Pastoral Development on the Northern California District.

Barry Huebner | Barry is a lay leader and serves as acting Chairperson of the District Advisory Board of the Chicago Central District.

Rev. Manoj Ingle | Manoj is a member of the USA/Canada Church Planting Task Force and serves the church in Wasilla, Alaska.

Rev. Kevin Jack | Kevin serves on the Large Launch Church Planting Task Force for the USA/Canada Region and as Lead Pastor of Be Hope Church in Beavercreek, Ohio.

Rev. Corey Jones | Corey serves as pastor of Crossroads Tabernacle in Fort Worth, Texas, and founder of The Awakening, a prayer movement that gathers 1,300+ Nazarenes annually from 35 different states.

Rev. Wynne Lankford | Wynne serves as the Lead Pastor at Southside Church located in Richmond, Virginia.

Dr. Adam Lewis | Adam serves as the Lead Pastor at Decatur First Nazarene located in Decatur, Illinois.

Dr. Mark Lindstrom | Mark serves as Superintendent of the North Arkansas District (South Central USA Field) on the USA/Canada Region.

Dr. Bob Mahaffey	Bob serves as Superintendent of the South-western Ohio District (East Central USA Field) on the USA/Canada Region.
Dr. Greg Mason	Greg serves as Superintendent of the North Carolina District (Southeast USA Field) on the USA/Canada Region.
Dr. Ron McCormick	Ron serves as Superintendent of the East Tennessee District (Southeast USA Field) on the USA/Canada Region.
Dr. Larry McKain	Larry serves as Superintendent of the Chicago Central District (Central USA Field) on the USA/Canada Region and was a founding member of the NewStart Task Force established by Dr. Bill Sullivan.
Dr. Dave McKellips	Dave serves as Superintendent of the Northeast Oklahoma District (South Central USA Field) on the USA/Canada Region.
Rev. Andy Monnin	Andy serves on the Large Launch Church Planting Task Force and as Lead Pastor of The Valley Church in Piqua, Ohio.
Rev. Lynnlee Moser	Lynnlee serves as Director of NexGen and The Collective, a USA/Canada Region initiative to mobilize a new generation of university students for church planting involvement.
Dr. Keith Newman	Keith serves as President of Southern Nazarene University located in Bethany, Oklahoma, and was a founding member of the NewStart Task Force established by Dr. Bill Sullivan.

Rev. Steve Ottley

Steve serves as Superintendent of the Canada Central District (Canada Field) on the USA/ Canada Region.

Dr. Mike Palmer

Mike serves as Superintendent of the Missouri District (North Central USA Field) on the USA/ Canada Region.

Dr. Jerry Porter

Jerry is a retired General Superintendent and currently serves the church as a missionary in a creative access Muslim country.

Dr. Brian Powell

Brian serves as Superintendent of the Kentucky District (Southeast USA Field) on the USA/ Canada Region.

Dr. Scott Rainey

Scott serves as the Global Director of the SDMI (Sunday School and Discipleship Ministries International).

Dr. Stan Reeder

Formally Superintendent of the Oregon Pacific District, Stan is the USA/Canada Director for Vibrant Church Renewal and serves as a Re-vitalizing Consultant to churches and districts.

Rev. Phil Rhoades

Phil serves as Superintendent of the Joplin District (North Central USA Field) on the USA/Canada Region.

Rev. Ron Riddle

Ron serves as Lead Pastor of Crossroads Cowboy Church in El Paso, Arkansas.

Rev. Dave Roberts

Dave serves as Lead Pastor of Montrose Church located in Montrose, California.

Dr. Jeren Rowell

Jeren serves as President of Nazarene Theological Seminary and Professor of Pastoral Ministry.

Dr. Christian Sarmiento Christian serves as Director of the South America Region.

Rev. Dale Schaeffer Dale serves as Superintendent of the Florida District (Southeast USA Field) on the USA/Canada Region.

Dr. Scott Sherwood Scott serves as Superintendent of the North-western Illinois District (Central USA Field) on the USA/Canada Region.

Rev. Kim Smith Kim serves as Superintendent of the Iowa District (North Central USA Field) on the USA/Canada Region.

Dr. Jeff Stark Jeff serves as a professor at Olivet Nazarene University, as Mission Strategy Team Leader on the Chicago Central District and as the Leader of the Reach77 Network in Chicago.

Dr. Brian Wangler Brian serves as Lead Pastor of Chicago First Church.

Rev. Kerry Willis Kerry serves as Superintendent of the Philadel-phia District (Eastern USA Field) on the USA/Canada Region.

Rev. David Wine David serves as a professor at Olivet Nazarene University and Small Groups Pastor at Gather-ing Point Church on the Chicago Central District.

Dr. Keith Wright Keith was a long-time serving Superintendent of the Kansas City District and now serves as a mentor to church leaders in retirement.

Rev. Doug Wyatt Doug serves as Superintendent of the Eastern Kentucky District (East Central USA Field) on the USA/Canada Region.

Preface

Why and How the MULTIPLYNAZ Series Has Emerged

There are several reasons we feel now is the time for a book series like this to be written for the church. The Scriptures tell us, "There is a time for everything and a season for every activity" (Ecclesiastes 3:1). We believe the Church of the Nazarene is one of the best kept secrets in the world, and that if more people only knew **what** we were doing, **why** we were doing it, and **how** we were doing it, the response would be overwhelming! When we started the writing project, none of us were smart enough to see the big picture. As the project evolved, we identified the things that would be helpful to discuss.

We first began by spilling all kinds of ideas on paper without paying attention to who the audience would be. After the initial book ideas were shared, feedback from multiple church leaders quickly moved the project from one **MULTIPLYNAZ** book to multiple books in a series. The different books flow from the suggestion of multiple leaders to address different audiences and subjects. As of this writing, the following books have emerged, with more to come as the Lord provides inspiration, time, and energy.

Book One—Fueling the Nazarene Movement with Love
> (focus) Foundations for Spiritual Movements
> (audience) Designed for everyone

Book Two—Fueling the Nazarene Movement with Healthy,
> **Multiplying Churches**
> (focus) Local Church Health and Church Development
> (audience) Local Pastors and Lay Leaders

**Book Three—Fueling the Nazarene Movement with Church
        Development Plans**
    (focus) Local Church Health and Church Development
    (audience) Local Pastors and Lay Leaders

Book Four—Fueling the Nazarene Movement with Healthy Districts
    (focus) District Health and District Development Plans
    (audience) Superintendents and District Leaders

While the writing of the **MULTIPLYNAZ** series has begun, it is **not** complete. We want this book series to be written, not just by an individual, but **by the church.** If we could, we would have EVERY pastor and lay leader participate in its writing. The church does not belong to a few, it belongs to everyone. Everyone should write the story, and everybody is—all over the world. We wish we could publish every miracle that is happening now in our 30,000+ congregations. Below is the list of objectives that have guided the **why** and **how** of these books emerging to their current form.

There are instructions on page 140 of this book that explain how **you can participate** by going to www.multiplynaz.org and offering your suggestions and corrections. Thanks in advance for **your contribution** to make the series better. As of this writing, the following are some of the issues the **MULTIPLYNAZ** series hopes to address.

Who We Are

The Nazarene Story: We wanted to tell the Nazarene story from a different perspective. We believe the church has both biblical and historical roots that especially outsiders and new people should know.

Joining the Movement of God through the People of God: We all believe God has given an inspiring vision to the church that we need to get behind and build agenda harmony with throughout the church. On 480+ districts, we can all participate!

Our Message—God's Perfect Love: We wanted to re-emphasize that beyond all accomplishments, the practice of God's love is the main message of our movement. We always want to lead with love.

Communicating Movement Momentum: Not enough Nazarenes know how well the church is expanding. As the world continues to shrink because of technology, we wanted to do a better job of sharing our evangelism and church planting success. Two million new believers will be joining the church in just the coming few years. We want to better communicate with each of them as they join our family, so they can more effectively fuel the movement where they serve.

Operating Among All Countries Equally: Unlike American businesses, our church has intentionally chosen a path of internationalization where we operate among ALL countries equally, including many of the poorest countries of the world. Our decisions as a church are not based on economic but on Kingdom values.

Biblical Roots for Being Connectional: Especially for a new generation coming into the church, we wanted to provide both biblical and practical reasons why Nazarenes choose to practice interdependence with each other as an emerging global family of believers.

Writing Project

Multiple Leaders Participating: There are 60+ participants in this project to date. We believe there will be many more who will read and give feedback. Every one of our 30,000+ pastors are heroes, serving the church in a local setting somewhere in one of the six regions of the world. As a team, we have written about the movement of God through the people of God because without exception, the church has been used by God to change our lives. It is an incredible privilege to serve the church and to participate in this greatest of opportunities to change the world.

No Individual Profit: Many books written by an individual are completed, shipped to a printer, printed, and then sold for a profit. This series of books is different. They are being printed at cost. No individual will profit from the books. When the books are sold, all proceeds will go to help the church better serve the world. The books' price tag is only used to establish value not to create compensation for writing.

Draft-Mode Feedback: We are doing "print on demand" while still in draft mode with the books in this series. We plan to distribute these copies to leaders who have not yet read that particular book and from whom we deeply desire input. We anticipate continued changes as more people read and offer their feedback. The purpose of draft mode printing is to allow participation and opportunity for ongoing feedback by every reader.

Feedback/Changes Welcomed from Everyone: We think the **MULYIPLYNAZ** series will be finished only when Nazarene leaders from around the world have the chance to read and offer their input to make the series better. We believe the series should be corrected and improved by the global church. We welcome ALL input and feedback because we know that none of us are smart enough to know everything we need to know to move the church forward with the spiritual momentum only the Holy Spirit can create.[1] This writing project needs and will take EVERYONE's input.

Building Agenda Harmony

The Value of Both Small and Large Churches: Because large churches are at a different place in their church development journey than smaller churches, we wanted to highlight the value of large churches, celebrate their contribution to our movement and multiply their influence. At the same time, we also want to emphasize the incredible contribution that small churches make to our movement. It takes **all kinds of churches** in all kinds of places to reach all kinds of people. We are learning that in many places, smaller is better. But we believe **every church** of every size matters!

Loving the Imperfect Church: We wanted to emphasize that the church Jesus founded was very imperfect, yet his vision motivated him to "give himself up" for the church (Ephesians 5:25-27). We believe each of us within the church should follow his example and have this same commitment.

Corporate Sanctification: We have watched churches practice corporate sanctification time and time again throughout our lives. We wanted to put language to what God was doing throughout the world in the Church of the Nazarene, linking sanctification with multiplication as Jesus did. We also wanted to emphasize that small churches in the process of closing can practice corporate sanctification and multiply into the next generation! We believe it is impossible to kill the influence of a local church, even when it closes. We serve the Lord of the church and his influence is eternal.

Value of the World Evangelism Fund: Not every country of the world has been blessed with the same financial resources. The early church modeled giving between churches (Acts 11:29-30), supported itinerant overseers like Paul, Titus, etc. (Philippians 4:15-18), and we do the same. The World Evangelism Fund is crucial for supporting the expansion and delivery of the church's work globally.

The Role of Districts: We wanted to look at the biblical foundations of districts, highlight what districts do, how districts can better practice interdependence,[2] why they provide training and how districts can decentralize to multiply.

Agenda Harmony with Jesus: We wanted to foster a greater understanding of the value of agenda harmony, how gaining it leads to spiritual breakthroughs, its biblical foundation, and the benefits of every local church and district working together to build it. We wanted to describe what our churches might look like if we put aside local and individual agendas and collectively sought only the agenda of Jesus for both the local and global impact of the church. This is a process that takes time and a willingness to regularly change our way of thinking.

Contagious Culture: We wanted every church in every district to discover the benefits of building a contagious culture and to provide an understanding of how this can happen, along with practical tools pastors and districts can use.

Evangelism/Disciple-Making

Renewing Our Outsider Passion: Our church has always had a heart for evangelism, church planting, and reaching those outside the Kingdom. As the church gets bigger, it becomes easier for this passion for outsiders to be replaced with other things. We wanted this book to be a call "back to our first love" of Jesus and his agenda. We wanted "to repent and do the things we did at first" (Revelation 2:4-5), always reminding ourselves of the "movement" days of the church. We never want to let "the movement days" among us die! We want to keep "fanning into flame the gift of God" (2 Timothy 1:6) we have received to fuel our passion for outsiders.

Disciple-Making—a Journey of Grace: Just like Christian parenting, we believe disciple-making begins at conception, not conversion. We believe in prevenient grace, saving grace, sanctifying grace, and growth in grace. We believe every person's entire disciple-making journey is **a journey of grace**.

Characteristics of Outsider-Focused Churches: We wanted to make widely available a study of the characteristics of outsider-focused churches. These characteristics include: 1) high expectations, 2) understanding spiritual realities, 3) being hospitable, 4) being guest-friendly, and 5) having outsider passion.

Every Church Encouraged to Build Disciple-Making "Next Steps": We wanted to both educate and encourage every Nazarene church to think through its disciple-making process and develop a simple series of "next steps" that new people can understand and follow when they first come into the church.

Reaching Cities: We all know the future will be different than the past. In 1800, only 3% of the world's population lived in cities. When the Church of the Nazarene began, the world was still primarily rural. Now 55% live in an urban area and 68% will live in a city in the coming decades.[3] Mega cities of the world (10 million+ people) are increasing in number. Every Nazarene, even those who live in rural areas, should be aware of the changing impact of cities on the world and join in prayer that God will help the church make Christlike disciples in the cities of all nations.

Church Planting/Church Development

Church Minimums: We wanted to re-emphasize our doctrine of the church, that it exists in many culturally conditioned forms and to create tools that will help existing churches and leaders discover nontraditional forms of church that the Lord is creating among us.

Everyone Learning to Think Like a Missionary: Every person who lives in a country where the Church of the Nazarene is located (160+ countries) **now** lives on a mission field. Every country of the world is **now** a mission field country! We wanted to re-emphasize the importance of every person in every church learning to think like a missionary, which includes planting microchurches and other forms of nontraditional churches as fast as we can, wherever we can.

Every Church Healthy and Multiplying: We believe, regardless of size, every church can be healthy and multiplying. Many churches multiply but do not realize it when it happens. We want "multiply language" to become the norm throughout the church. Small churches that do micro multiplication by starting a new ministry or experience God raising up a new leader—these are multiplying churches.

Micro and Macro Multiplication: We wanted every church to be educated in the understanding of both micro and macro multiplication. Many church leaders are only familiar with macro multiplication (church planting), because it is more visible on districts. The practice of micro multiplication is foundational to developing healthy, multiplying churches.

Pathway to Planting: We wanted to listen to feedback and then develop a Nazarene Pathway to Planting. We believe 1) Prayer, 2) God's Call, 3) Orientation, 4) Assessment, 5) Training, 6) Church Development Plan, and 7) Mentors will make a long-term difference in the quality of church planting on every district throughout the world.

Large Launch Church Planting: We wanted to introduce the multiplication of large church plants, campuses, etc. as one of a number of church planting models. We wanted to share the values of **MULTI-PLYNAZ** (including residencies) and cast a vision for intermediate and large churches launching dozens of large launch churches, multi-sites, campuses, etc. in the days ahead.

Seeking to Improve:

Spiritual Planning: We wanted to introduce the process of spiritual planning to every Nazarene church, explain **why** both **prayer** and **planning** are important, and offer simple tools to churches that desire help in building a Church Development Plan they update annually.[4] This would include identifying church life-cycle issues, building a shared vision, building agenda harmony, spiritual momentum, etc. A lack of planning is usually a major cause of church development failure.

Mobilizing Our Universities and Schools: Over 51,000 students currently attend our Nazarene educational institutions globally, and too many of them do not know the Nazarene story, how exciting it is, how the church is positioned to change the world, and how they can play a vital part in shaping the church's future. Not only must we engage with these passionate students, we must also better engage with visionary university professors who are shaping the future of the church in their classrooms.

Mobilizing Kingdom-Minded Lay Leaders: Many sharp, gifted lay leaders among us are yet to be mobilized for our movement in local churches, on districts, and globally. Especially needed are leaders with Kingdom hearts and business minds gifted to serve the church in the marketplaces of the world. Through **MARKETPLACENAZ,** we wanted to communicate with these gifted lay leaders the church has an opportunity for them to come help change the world!

Organized into Regions, Fields and Districts: We wanted every church leader reading this series to understand the incredible development of the global church. Many of our pastors and lay leaders are so immersed in their own setting, they have yet to discover everything good that is happening! The General Board of the church has wisely organized the church into regions, fields, and districts. As the world shrinks with technology and global communication expands, every Nazarene needs a fresh, new understanding of the global network we already have in place to achieve the mission of the church.

Clarifying USA/Canada Region Fields: Since being announced as a mission field in 1989, districts and churches on the USA/Canada Region have continued to learn what this means. While the Region has been informally organized into "fields," more Nazarenes need to understand the big picture of how USA/Canada fits into the global regions of the world and the other fields we have. Clarifying these will help Nazarenes everywhere better embrace the global vision of the church.

A Book Designed for Individuals New to the Church: Too many times, we are guilty of speaking and writing only for insiders in the church. We want to develop a book in this series that will be designed primarily for individuals who are just beginning to attend one of our churches and are investigating the Church of the Nazarene for the first time. As you read and explore the above reasons the **MULTIPLYNAZ** series is being written, we hope you will rediscover how marvelous this movement of God through the people of God has become, and you will fall in love with the church Jesus loves so much. If your devotion to Christ's Bride is rekindled and your love for the agenda of Jesus is deepened, our purpose will have been achieved. Our prayers are with you.

How To Use This Book

Early on in this writing project, our feedback told us we needed to make sure the books would be used in a group, not just read individually. This required us to be mindful of small groups, Sunday School classes, midweek gatherings or pastors' cohorts where people would come together to pray, read Scripture and discuss questions and ideas from the **MULTIPLYNAZ** series. We always had the early learning pattern of Jesus in mind as we wrote.

We know little about the preparation years of Jesus between his birth (Luke 2:1-20) and the beginning of his ministry (Luke 3:21-22). We know Jesus went to Egypt when he was young for a short time (Matthew 2:13-15) and then returned to Nazareth where he grew up (Matthew 2:19-22). This is where we get the name for our church, the Church of **the Nazarene** (Matthew 2:23).

The only other recorded childhood incidents we know about Jesus was that every year he attended the festival of the Passover in Jerusalem (Luke 2:41). Being raised in a devout Jewish home, there were multiple times Jesus went to Jerusalem for the Passover festival. When a Jewish boy turned twelve, he became a "son of the law," taking on the full obligations of what it meant to be a Jewish young man.

We don't know everything that happened to Jesus at this Passover festival when he was twelve, but we do know it was a BIG event with lots of relatives and friends. There were ceremonies, priests reading portions of the law in Hebrew, and Jesus most likely participated. There would have been a challenge to practice what he knew to be right, to be obedient to his parents, to be kind to his brothers and sisters, to help those in need and to be faithful to the God of Abraham, Isaac, and Jacob.

After the festival was over, Jesus' parents thought he was with all of their relatives and friends as the group started home to Nazareth, and they traveled a whole day without seeing him. When they discovered Jesus was missing, they went back to Jerusalem (Luke 2:42-45). Three days later they found Jesus doing two things—he was "sitting among the teachers, 1) **listening** to them and 2) **asking them questions**" (Luke 2:46).

This is the early learning pattern of Jesus—to listen and ask questions. Jesus practiced listening and asking questions throughout his life. We will always get the right answer to any problem we face if we follow his example and simply learn to ask the right question. Again, our feedback from leaders told us we should design the book to be used in groups, not just read individually.[5] Out of this feedback, the following are three "reader" questions we always kept in mind as we wrote:

1. What is the book saying?
2. What does this idea mean?
3. How can we use it in our church?

To help you as a reader better understand and facilitate a healthier use of the book, each chapter has a set of reflection questions, designed for use by pastor's cohorts, Sunday school classes, small groups, midweek gatherings, etc. Some questions on the contents and preface can be found on the next page.

Questions for Reflection—Contents & Preface

1. Do you think it is a good idea for a book to be written by the church for the church? Why or why not? How would you gather more and better ideas to make the **MULTIPLYNAZ** series better for the whole church to use?
2. The focus of this book series is healthy, multiplying churches. Within this focus, is there a subject or key issue that you feel is missing? If so, what is it?
3. As you read through the Preface which lists a number of issues the **MULTIPLYNAZ** series plans to address, what issue(s) stand out to you? Why?
4. As you read through the Preface, is there anything about the church you learned that you did not know before? If so, what?

Introduction
Welcome to the Church!

Jesus "went and lived in a town called Nazareth. So was
fulfilled what was said through the prophets,
that he would be called a Nazarene." (Matthew 2:23)

If you are new to our church like tens of thousands are throughout the world, you may be thinking to yourself, "What is a Nazarene?"
We call ourselves the Church of **the Nazarene** because we follow Jesus
the Nazarene who is the head of our church (Ephesians 4:15-16).

Even if people are not followers of Jesus, most today will acknowledge that Jesus Christ is the greatest leader who ever lived. His
coming to earth cuts our calendar in two. Every time we think about
what year it is, we are reminded of how many years it has been since
the Son of God entered the bloodstream of humanity. God became a human being (John 1:1-14), he was born into the world over 2,000 years
ago, and after living a few short years in Egypt (Matthew 2:19-22),
Jesus and his family moved to a town called Nazareth.

Jesus lived for 30 years in Nazareth before he began a three-
year teaching and preaching ministry (Luke 3:23). It is a historical fact
that he was crucified on a Roman cross and buried in a borrowed tomb;
three days later, Jesus rose from the dead, and today he is very much
alive!

This is the biblical foundation of the Church of "the Nazarene."
Our foundation as a church is built, not just on a theology or a history, but on a Person. In the Church of the Nazarene, we are not just a

denomination with great beliefs and tremendous associations. Our allegiance is not just to a human organization. We follow a person who is alive, the resurrected Jesus. Every time you hear the words Church of the Nazarene, we hope you will first think about us as the church of **the Nazarene,** led by Jesus! Our mission is to follow him, making Christlike disciples in every nation of the world.

> Every time you hear the words Church of the Nazarene, we hope you will first think about us as the Church of **the Nazarene**, led by Jesus!

Our church name has both biblical and historical roots. There are twelve times in the New Testament we find a reference to the Nazarenes.[1] In the Bible, before the followers of Jesus were called Christians, they were referred to as the "Nazarenes." Here are four of these references. First, prophets called Jesus a Nazarene. Jesus "went and lived in a town called Nazareth. So was fulfilled what was said through the prophets, that he would be called a Nazarene" (Matthew 2:23).

Secondly, the apostle Paul was a leader of "Nazarene" churches. When Paul was in Caesarea and brought before Governor Felix, "some of the elders and a lawyer named Tertullus brought charges against Paul before the governor" (Acts 24:1). Their accusation was, "We have found this man to be a troublemaker...and a ringleader of the Nazarene" movement (Acts 24:5).

Thirdly, the night that Jesus was disowned by Peter, "one of the servant girls of the high priest came by" (Mark 14:66). She looked closely at Peter standing by the fire and said, "You also were with that Nazarene, Jesus" (Mark 14:67).

Fourthly, on the morning of the greatest event in human history, at the empty tomb it was an angel from heaven who said to the women,

"You are looking for Jesus the Nazarene? He is not here. He is risen!" (Mark 16:6) The movement of God through the people of God is not centered in just an organization but in a person—**Jesus the Nazarene!**

The Church of the Nazarene today is part of the long history of the church over the past 2,000 years. We identify with the historic church in preaching the Word, administering the sacraments and calling people to live holy lives in full devotion to God.

> In the Bible, before the followers of Jesus were called Christians, they were referred to as "Nazarenes."

In 18th century England, through the preaching of John and Charles Wesley, tens of thousands of people turned from sin and were empowered for Christian service.[2] John Wesley's teaching from the Bible included a call for Christians to not only accept Jesus as their Savior, but also to yield their lives fully to him, what Wesley called "entire sanctification."

Another way to describe this is to be totally committed in your life to the agenda of Jesus, not your own agenda. The apostle Paul explains it as God promising to "sanctify us through and through" until our whole spirit, soul, and body is filled with the Holy Spirit and our agenda becomes the agenda of Jesus (1 Thessalonians 5:23-24). Entire sanctification to "the whole will of God" (Acts 20:27) is the distinctive teaching of our church and the commitment of Nazarenes around the world.

It is also the biblical key to multiplying the church. The word sanctify means "to be set apart, purified for God's purpose." When an individual is sanctified, they become totally devoted to Jesus and his agenda. When a local church is sanctified, the church becomes totally devoted to Jesus and his agenda as well. The church is no longer just concerned about itself. It is willing to sacrifice part or all of itself to multiply the Kingdom (John 12:24).

> When a local church is sanctified, the church is willing to sacrifice part or all of itself to multiply the Kingdom.

The reason we use the term **MULTIPLYNAZ** is because the Church of the Nazarene is a movement of God through the people of God who are committed to multiply. We are a movement with a focus on outsiders. We are a movement that challenges people to be sanctified, and local churches to be sanctified as well. When churches are sanctified, they see beyond themselves and their own setting. While they serve the Kingdom locally, they see the vision of Jesus globally, to "go and make disciples of all nations" (Matthew 28:19).

Through the united vision of these local churches, the Church of the Nazarene has been able to expand internationally at an exponential rate. From modest beginnings in 1908, the church has multiplied into 160+ countries of the world. This includes a number of countries where the church operates underground and leaders share the gospel at great personal risk. Weekly, in the Church of the Nazarene, we start 27 new churches. As of this writing, weekly we have 2,872 new people join the church. Nazarene churches have been multiplying at this rate every week for the last 10 years!

> There is a movement of church leaders God is raising up among us who are committed to multiply.

We welcome you to this movement of God through the people of God. We have no doubt the day will come soon when 3,000 people will join the church through the Church of the Nazarene **every week**, the same number of people who joined the church on the day of Pentecost! (Acts 2:41) We are not the only church; we are part of what Jesus is doing through so many churches, in so many places.

> Weekly, we start 27 new churches and 2,872 new people join the church. Nazarene churches have been multiplying at this rate **every week** for the last 10 years!

Throughout the world, people follow Jesus and begin attending his church one by one. He knows every person inside our church by name. He knows the name of every person outside as well. According to the United Nations, the global population will reach eight billion by 2024 and likely reach nine billion by 2042. While Jesus has a close relationship with and provides personal care and love to every church member, we also believe Jesus wants us to leave our "four walls" and go out looking for the lost, looking for outsiders until we find them (Luke 15:4-7). He already knows their name, he knows where they live (Acts 17:26), and he wants to introduce us to them! When Jesus meets them, he welcomes these outsiders with open arms, just like he would a lost son who has been found by his father (Luke 15:17-32). He brings them home and then he throws a party. This is the agenda of Jesus—and because it is his agenda, we have made it our agenda as well.

God does not have a mission for the church. God has a church for his mission. We are unashamedly a church that lives that mission, bearing witness in both word and deed to those disconnected from faith, void of hope and unaware of God's love for them (1 Corinthians 13:13). Jesus came to earth for outsiders. We know there are limitations with language referring to people as outsiders, the lost, etc., depending on the culture we are in. We wish we could find the perfect words to use with each audience we have. It is love that guides us. The Bible says, "God so loved the world that he gave his one and only Son" (John 3:16). The promise to Abraham was that "all people on earth would be blessed

> The agenda of Jesus is to welcome outsiders, and because it is his agenda, we have made it our agenda as well.

through him" (Genesis 12:3). The prophets regularly reminded the Jewish people that God's plan of salvation included outsiders (Jonah 4:11), and that plan involved the whole world (Isaiah 45:22). During his earthly ministry Jesus regularly affirmed that "he came to seek and to save the lost" (Luke 19:10).

One of our favorite descriptions of Jesus is "a friend of sinners" (Matthew 11:19). It reveals the compassionate heart of Jesus for those who feel far from God. Our Lord was a personal friend to sinners before they were ever aware he could also be their personal savior. This title was not initially intended to be a compliment. It was an insult from religious people who did not like Jesus' ethics or his theology.[3]

A key group of religious leaders in Jesus' day were called Pharisees. They were supposed to teach God's law to the people. The tax collectors and sinners were not welcomed by the Pharisees. When Jesus gathered all these outsiders around him (Luke 15:1), building relationships with them and eating in their homes (Matthew 9:9-13), the religious people complained, "This man welcomes sinners and eats with them" (Luke 15:2). Jesus did not focus his agenda on these religious people. In fact, most of the harsh things Jesus had to say was to them. The agenda of Jesus was always "the outsiders."

If you are reading this book, you were once an outsider to the church. Even the Apostle Paul was an outsider. We all were once outsiders. Here is the good news! "But now in Christ Jesus you who were

once far away [outsiders], **have been brought near** through the blood of Christ...he himself is our peace...he has **destroyed the barrier,** the **dividing wall**...He came and preached peace to you who were far away...Consequently, you are no longer foreigners and aliens but fellow citizens with God's people and members of God's household...In him, you are being built together to become a dwelling in which God lives by his Spirit" (Ephesians 2:13-22). Now you are part of the movement of God through the people of God. Welcome to the church!

> Now you are part of the movement of God through the people of God. Welcome to the church!

Questions for Reflection—Introduction

1. What raised your interest concerning the biblical and historical roots of the Church of the Nazarene and the life of Jesus?
2. Did you learn anything you did not know before? What was new to you? Who will you share your learning with?
3. As a Christian, how often do you think about the global movement of God and what Jesus is doing to expand his church around the world? Do you think you should think about "the world" more often than you do? Why? (John 3:16)
4. "God does not have a mission for the church. God has a church for his mission." What do you think about this statement? Do you agree with it? Why or why not?

5. "Jesus came to earth for outsiders." Any language we use for the people we love and want to reach is inadequate. How would you describe the mission of Jesus to reach those who have not yet come to faith?

6. The book mentions a number of biblical references that indicate the focus of both God in the Old Testament and Jesus in the New Testament is reaching outsiders who are separate from him and his church. Do you agree with this? Why?

7. Does the agenda of your church have more of a focus on "insiders" or "outsiders?" Why do you think this is? What do you feel Jesus thinks about this? If needed, discuss ways your focus could change.

8. As you began reading this book, is there anything Jesus whispered to you that he wants you to think about? To reflect on? Who will you share your spiritual learning with?

Book One—
Foundations for
Spiritual Movements

1

A Great Future Together

"So I prophesied as he commanded me, and breath entered them; they came to life and stood up on their feet—a vast army." (Ezekiel 37:10)

We hear the sounds of a new movement coming! The sounds are not that of congregations that continue to "do church" as they have always done before. The sounds we hear are the marching of those who hear the beat of a different drum. They are the innovators, the risk-takers, the ones anxious for adventure.

> They believe every Nazarene church can become a healthy, multiplying church regardless of size.

Many of them are new to the Church of the Nazarene. They know they are called, spiritually gifted and led by God. They include both clergy and lay leaders. They are a growing group of people within a global movement. They are a movement of servant leaders scattered in 30,000+ Nazarene churches throughout the world.

The people in this movement are different from members of status quo churches. They never stop learning, are mentally growing, and changing. They are beginning to understand what is crucial to the long-term health and growth of Christ's church. **They believe every Nazarene church can become a healthy, multiplying church regardless of size**. Like Jesus, they have a heart for outsiders. Some of them are developing a distinctive mix of spiritual gifts that God has uniquely given them, in order to multiply the entry points into Christ's Kingdom.

They have a heart for evangelism, church planting, mentoring new leaders, multiplying new campuses, new churches, etc. Their thinking and actions help create the culture that fuels the Nazarene movement.

Discontented with status quo and ordinary church routine, they feel the same urge as was felt in the heart of the apostle Paul. "It has always been my ambition to preach the gospel where Christ was not known, so that I would not be building on someone else's foundation" (Romans 15:20). They focus on those outside the Kingdom. They keep encouraging their local church to focus on outsiders, people beyond the four walls of the church (Matthew 18:10-14) who have not yet come to faith in Christ. They "have a deep love for unbelievers," believing they are lost and need to be found.[1]

Another characteristic of people in this movement is that they understand their work often goes unnoticed. When the gospel made its greatest advance in the book of Acts, non-Jews (men from Cyprus and Cyrene) went to Antioch and spoke to Greeks about Jesus (Acts 11:20). Many people have heard about Paul and Barnabas being sent as the first church planting leaders from Antioch (Acts 13:2-3). But who started the Antioch church? We do not even know their names. But we do know "the Lord's hand was with them and a great number of people in Antioch believed," so the "Jerusalem ministry center" sent Barnabas down to find out what was going on (Acts 11:21-22).

> The ultimate purpose of life within the church is to bring glory to God.

Where multiplying movements happen, there are always scores of unnamed people working behind the scenes. They get little credit or recognition for their labor. But when they see the Savior, they will hear him say, "Well done, good and faithful servant" (Matthew 25:21,23). For them, that is enough because their ultimate purpose in life is to bring glory to God (Romans 5:2, 8:17).

Whether you are reading this book individually or discussing these ideas within a group, you will soon discover the attitudes, spirit and heart of everyone involved. Paul instructs us, "So ... whatever you do, do it all for the glory of God" (1 Corinthians 10:31). God created everything to reflect his glory.

Jesus' great desire was to bring glory to God. The night before Jesus died, he prayed to his Father, "I have brought you glory on earth by completing the work you gave me to do" (John 17:4). As a team, our desire is to do the same—to complete the work God has given us to do. "We are God's handiwork, created in Christ Jesus to do good works, which God prepared in advance for us to do" (Ephesians 2:10). "Now to him who is able to do immeasurably more than all we ask or imagine...**to him be glory in the church** and in Christ Jesus throughout all generations, for ever and ever! Amen" (Ephesians 3:20-21). We believe the ultimate purpose of our lives in the church is to bring glory to God.

This is a book about how we can better fuel our Nazarene movement. There are numerous books today on church theology and strategies. We have training programs that highlight starting new churches, revitalizing existing congregations, etc. New strategies continue to emerge as the church finds better ways of fueling the movement of God through the people of God. As a team of 480+ districts, we are getting better at providing specialized training for church leaders. The premise of this book, however, is that to keep fueling the Nazarene movement, we need more than strategies and training.

We believe the Holy Spirit is bringing us together. We share a common agenda. We enjoy a spiritual unity that Jesus talked about (John 17:21-23). We know multiplying movements require church leaders to work closely together. The **desire** to fuel the movement, the **resources** needed, and the right **climate** are being created among us.

Our movement aims to plant all kinds of churches in all kinds of places to reach all kinds of people. Our movement believes EVERY church can participate! This is the objective this book seeks to support.

As Nazarenes, we know what we believe about the church will affect how we behave within the church. Our movement operates with a biblical understanding of the church. We choose to love the church as Jesus loves it (Ephesians 5:25-27). We understand for any multiplying movement of God to be sustained, we must regularly clarify our theology and understanding of the church.

> The desire to fuel the movement, the resources needed and the right climate are being created among us.

God is glorified and **his mission in the world advances greatly** when groups of churches lock arms together in his name to multiply his Kingdom. When God's people enjoy unity and agenda harmony, they are unstoppable! David writes, "How good and pleasant it is when God's people live together in unity" (Psalm 133:1). "For there the Lord bestows his blessing, even life forevermore" (Psalm 133:3). Our churches and districts throughout the world are gaining agenda harmony! What is agenda harmony? Let's define it.

Agenda: "an outline or plan of the things that must be done"
Harmony: "a unified arrangement of parts with a common focus"

Putting these two words together, **agenda harmony** occurs when the members of a local church, district, field, or region work together for a common objective, with a common purpose, in a common spirit.

The apostle Paul knew the importance of agenda harmony within the church and wrote, "If you have any fellowship with the Spirit… then make my joy complete by being like-minded, having the same love, being one in spirit and purpose" (Philippians 2:1-2). How good and pleasant it is when churches have these four characteristics. They are: 1) like-minded, 2) have the same love, 3) one in spirit, and 4) one in purpose.

> The Lord bestows his blessing where there is unity and agenda harmony.

As a team of leaders, we believe this is not just a suggestion or an option to God. "The Lord bestows his blessing, even everlasting life" (Psalm 133:3), **only** where there is **unity** and **agenda harmony.** Only where people are one in spirit and have the same love will we see lost and broken people come to Christ. It is when local churches, districts, fields and regions are "brought to complete unity that the world will know" Christ's church as he designed us to be (John 17:23). We do not contend for unity in local style or strategy, but unity through our shared commitments to interdependence and the agenda of Jesus.[2]

Paul urges church leaders to "make every effort to keep the unity of the Spirit through the bond of peace" (Ephesians 4:2). Unity of the Spirit does not mean uniformity. We can walk hand in hand without always seeing eye to eye. We operate locally and interdependently within districts to build healthy, multiplying Nazarene churches. The health and mission of God's church always **begins** with our local church. But at the same time, the vision of Jesus is much bigger than each local church. What is at stake is the salvation of the planet—"Judea, Samaria and the ends of the earth" (Acts 1:8). Jesus gives **every Christian** the commission to "go and make disciples of **all nations**" (Matthew 28:19). This includes both the people who live around us and those who

live around the world. The Nazarene multiplying movement is a movement of God through the people of God. From humble beginnings, it
now spans 160+ countries globally, with 480+ districts, on 41 fields, in
6 world regions. Through a combination of unity and agenda harmony,
Nazarenes have become a global community of believers that has led
hundreds of thousands of people throughout the world to faith and holy
living. Fueling this movement of God has required agenda harmony
among local congregations and the districts and fields with which they
are connected.

> Fueling the movement of God requires agenda harmony among local congregations and the districts with which they are connected.

We desire the following four ideas to shape the spirit of the **MULTIPLYNAZ** series: 1) God is at work raising up a new movement of church leaders who focus on those outside the church. 2) Much
of their work will go unnoticed. 3) Their ultimate purpose is to bring
glory to God. 4) Agenda harmony is required for God's continued
blessings on a local church, district, field or region.

Discussions about church multiplication quickly lead us into a
discussion of strategy. This book will deal with some lessons we are
learning about effective strategy. We need solid strategies for starting
new churches and revitalizing existing churches. But we are learning
that no matter how good the strategy, it will never make its desired impact unless we keep fueling agenda harmony.

A healthy new church, revitalized church or revitalized district
happens when leaders of the church are able to gain agenda harmony.
**Gaining agenda harmony is where every healthy church or district
experiences their breakthrough.** We believe this is what happened to
the disciples of Jesus through believing prayer on the day of Pentecost.

"When the day of Pentecost came, they were all together in one place" (Acts 2:1). We believe great agenda harmony is never gained through strategy. Churches struggle when strategy alone is their focus. We are learning that agenda harmony is gained "as the Body of Christ is called together by the Holy Spirit" through the power of Scripture. As Nazarenes, we declare, "We believe in the Church, the community that confesses Jesus Christ as Lord...the Body of Christ called together by the Holy Spirit **through the Word**" (Articles of Faith, Manual, par 11). We believe the Holy Spirit alone creates, sustains and unifies the church.

> No matter how good the strategy, it will never make its desired impact unless we keep fueling agenda harmony.

Agenda harmony grows when we share a biblical understanding of the church. Spiritual power and spiritual results come through the work of the Holy Spirit as he reminds us of the Word among us (John 1:1,14, 14:26). It is the power of Scripture, not just strategy, which shapes the culture of leaders' hearts and fuels agenda harmony bringing transformation in people's lives, both inside and outside the church.

This book is about the foundations of spiritual movements. What we believe greatly impacts how we behave. The prayer of our team is that as you read this book, you will see and love the church as Jesus does in fresh, new ways. He literally "gave himself up for her" (Ephesians 5:25). He expects us to do the same. Our desire is that God

> Great agenda harmony is never gained through strategy. It is only gained "as the body of Christ is called together by the Holy Spirit" through the power of Scripture.

will take these pages and use them for the multiplication of his church, "until the earth is filled with the knowledge of the glory of the Lord, as the waters cover the sea," (Habakkuk 2:14) and "the kingdom of the world has become the kingdom of our Lord and of his Christ, and he reigns for ever and ever" (Revelation 11:15). Our prayers are with you.[3]

Questions for Reflection—Chapter 1

1. Do you feel you are part of the movement the book talks about where people never stop learning and are mentally growing and changing? Do you want to be? Why or why not?

2. Do you believe every Nazarene church can become a healthy, multiplying church regardless of size? Why or why not?

3. Are you the kind of person that likes the "status quo" and "ordinary church routine" or are you the kind of person who would like to see the church change in some ways? Why or why not?

4. Before reading this book, how familiar were you with "the Nazarene movement" that now has 480+ districts around the world?

5. How does being part of this kind of a movement make you feel? Do you believe the church you attend can participate in and become a more active, vital part of the Nazarene movement? Why or why not?

6. Before reading this book, have you ever heard of the term "agenda harmony?" When?

7. Have you ever read or thought deeply about the spiritual truth behind Psalm 133:1,3 and Philippians 2:1-2? How does unity and agenda harmony make God's church unstoppable? Discuss your thoughts with a cohort, small group or class.

8. How would your church act differently if everyone in the church experienced agenda harmony? What would look different? What would be different? What would probably need to change? How would you know when agenda harmony had happened?

9. The book states, "It is the power of Scripture, not just strategy, which shapes the culture of leaders' hearts and fuels agenda harmony bringing transformation in people's lives." Do you believe this statement? Share your thoughts about this with others in the group.

10. Have you ever been part of a "spiritual movement?" Do you believe it is possible that "the earth can be filled with the knowledge of the glory of the Lord, as the waters cover the sea" (Habakkuk 2:14)? What would this look like?

2

The Greatest of These—Is Love

"A new command I give you: Love one another...By this everyone
will know that you are my disciples, if you love one another."
(John 13:34-35)

"And now these three remain: faith, hope and love. But the greatest of
these is love." (1 Corinthians 13:13)

Saul (the apostle Paul), who wrote almost half the New Testament, began as an outsider to the church. He did not begin his spiritual journey practicing what he wrote in 1 Corinthians 13. Saul began as a zealous Christian killer. He was a key influencer behind the death of Stephen (Acts 7:58). Following Stephen's death, Saul led a great persecution against the church.

"All the believers except the apostles were scattered throughout Judea and Samaria" (Acts 8:1). Luke tells us "Saul began to destroy the church. Going from house to house, he dragged off men and women and put them in prison" (Acts 8:3). On the road to Damascus, all that changed when Saul had a divine moment with God. A light from heaven flashed and a voice spoke, "Saul, Saul, why do you persecute **me**?...**I am Jesus**, whom you are persecuting" (Acts 9:4-5).

We are very careful with our attitudes toward the church because of what the Scriptures teach us about the church. In the paragraph above, did you catch the inescapable link? Saul was persecuting the church (Acts 8:3) and trying to destroy the church. But in Acts chapter 9, Jesus makes clear Saul is not just persecuting an imperfect group of people. When he speaks badly, hurts with his words and actions, or when his attitudes toward the church are wrong, Saul hears a voice: "**I am Jesus** whom you are persecuting."

The teaching of the Scripture is clear. In God's eyes, any wrong I do to the church, I do to Jesus. This same zealous Christian killer later writes, "This is a profound mystery, but Christ and his church have become one flesh" (Ephesians 5:30-31). What an attitude change he had! When he met Jesus, Saul dramatically changed his attitude toward the church.

> In God's eyes, any wrong
> I do to the church,
> I do to Jesus.

That day on the Damascus road began a new journey in Saul's understanding of "ecclesiology."[1] Before he met Jesus, he didn't know who Jesus was. He didn't love Jesus, love outsiders or love the church that "Jesus gave himself up for" (Ephesians 5:25). He was yet to understand what fueled the movement that began in the Upper Room. Jesus told his disciples the night before he died, "A new command I give you: Love one another. As I have loved you, so you must love one another. By this **everyone will know that you are my disciples, if you love one another**" (John 13:34-35). Saul didn't know how to lead with love. He was a hard-driving apostle. Much like as in our lives today, love was something he had to learn. It no doubt took some time.

After Saul met Jesus, he knew Jesus was raised from the dead and was the long-awaited Messiah. So, this once zealous persecutor immediately became a zealous preacher, someone willing to openly debate about Jesus even in Jerusalem. Saul's hard-driving ways stirred up Jews to want to kill Christians even more (Acts 9:29). That led the Jerusalem church to send Saul back to his home in Tarsus, and only then did the church enjoy a time of peace (Acts 9:31).

As mentioned before, the gospel made its greatest advance

among non-Jews who went to Antioch and spoke to Greeks about Jesus (Acts 11:22). The Jerusalem church heard about the movement breaking out in Antioch. Someone was needed to lead this work, and they trusted Barnabas (Acts 11:20). When he arrived, "full of the Holy Spirit and faith...a great number of people were brought to the Lord" (Acts 11:24). Barnabas saw the spiritual potential for Kingdom growth and knew he could not lead alone. He needed help.

> It was Barnabas who rescued Saul to the church by bringing him to Antioch, mentoring him and giving him a place to serve.

Barnabas had seen latent talent in Saul when others didn't (Acts 9:27). He had seen Saul speak and thought he had potential to be a great leader for the Nazarene movement. So, Barnabas went to Tarsus to look for Saul and convinced him there was a place for him in the church. Some scholars think Saul may have been on the spiritual sidelines for eight years, left by a Jerusalem church who thought his personality was too "visionary" and confrontational (Acts 9:29-30). It was Barnabas who rescued Saul to the church by bringing him to Antioch, mentoring him and giving him a place to serve (Acts 11:25-26).

When Barnabas and Saul began their first missionary journey (Acts 13:2-3), Saul was probably still rough in his practice of the fruit of the Spirit (Galatians 5:22-23). While love was certainly part of his message, love was not Saul's greatest theme. In Cyprus, Paul (Saul's Roman name) called Elymas "a child of the devil and an enemy of everything that is right" (Acts 13:10). Being asked "to give a message of encouragement" in Pisidian Antioch (Acts 13:14-15), Paul spoke and warned the Jews not to be "scoffers, to wonder and perish" (Acts 13:41). After regional evangelism success (Acts 13:49), over time

Paul's preaching in Antioch "stirred up persecution and they were ex-pelled" (Acts 13:50). In Iconium there was "a plot to mistreat them and stone them" (Acts 14:5). In Lystra Paul was stoned, dragged out-side the city and left for dead (Acts 14:19). After the Jerusalem coun-cil, the harshness of Paul's attitude toward Mark caused "such a sharp disagreement with Barnabas that they parted company" (Acts 15:39). Paul later expressed a huge change in attitude toward Mark (2 Timothy 4:11).

Paul's early preaching method was this: "…he went into the synagogue, and on multiple Sabbath days, he reasoned with the Jews from the Scriptures, **explaining and proving** that the Messiah had to suffer and rise from the dead" (Acts 17:2-3). As Paul began preach-ing, his central themes were not wrong—the good news of the gos-pel, Jesus and the resurrection, Jesus as the promised Messiah, etc. As Paul walked daily with Jesus though, Paul's attitudes slowly began to change.

By his third missionary journey, about A.D. 55, Paul sat down and wrote a message he had missed at the beginning. Just like every church today, the Corinthian church needed agenda harmony. Paul be-gins his letter by writing, "I appeal to you, brothers and sisters, in the name of our Lord Jesus Christ, that all of you **agree with one another** so that there may be no divisions among you, and that you may be **per-fectly united** in mind and thought" (1 Corinthians 1:10).

Can you see Paul reflecting on what the Holy Spirit was teach-ing him about himself? After his initial preaching efforts were filled with confrontation and conflict, trying to argue and prove to Jews and Gentiles that they should become Christians, Paul experienced new in-spiration from the Holy Spirit. It was true! Jesus had promised, "The Holy Spirit will teach you all things and will **remind you of every-thing** I have said to you" (John 14:26).

At a writing table in Ephesus, Paul wrote a letter to the Corinthians about spiritual gifts and then he penned, "now I will show you **the most excellent way**" (1 Corinthians 12:31). The following words have fueled the movement of God through the people of God for the past 2,000 years.

"If I speak in the tongues of men or of angels, but do not have love, I am only a resounding gong or a clanging cymbal. If I have the gift of prophecy and can fathom all mysteries and all knowledge, and if I have a faith that can move mountains, but do not have love, I am nothing. If I give all I possess to the poor and surrender my body to the flames, but do not have love, I gain nothing.

> The words of First Corinthians 13 have fueled the movement of God through the people of God for the past 2,000 years.

Love is patient, love is kind. It does not envy, it does not boast, it is not proud. It is not rude, it is not self-seeking, it is not easily angered, it keeps no record of wrongs. Love does not delight in evil but rejoices with the truth. It always protects, always trusts, always hopes, always perseveres. Love never fails… And now these three remain: faith, hope and love. But the greatest of these is love" (1 Corinthians 13:1-8,13).

What is the message that fuels our movement? Jesus said the Greatest Commandment was "to love God with all your heart and love your neighbor as yourself" (Matthew 22:37,39). He said, "Everyone will know you are my disciples if you love one another" (John 13:35). From the beginning of our movement, the church's primary message has been a message of holy love. Here in 1 Corinthians 13, Paul gives five reasons why holy love is our main message.

First, without love, all that we **say** is **ineffective**. "If I speak in the tongues of men or of angels, but have not love, I am only a resounding gong or a clanging cymbal" (1 Corinthians 13:1). Words without love are empty, they are just noise. Words without love are nothing, they are fruitless. The Corinthians were caught up with speaking in tongues—proud of their spiritual eloquence. They declared, "We can speak in the tongues of men and angels." But Paul made the point, "You are majoring on the minors

> Without love, all that we say is ineffective and all that we know is incomplete.

because talking in tongues is nothing compared to love." Without love, all that we say is ineffective.

Secondly, without love, all that we **know** is **incomplete**. "If I have the gift of prophecy and can fathom all mysteries and all knowledge...but have not love, I am nothing" (1 Corinthians 13:2). We can have a college degree, a master's degree, or a doctor's degree. We can be a Bible genius, memorize and quote hundreds of Bible verses, but God says, all of that doesn't matter compared to love. "Knowledge puffs up, but love builds up" (1 Corinthians 8:1). Without love, all that we know is incomplete.

Thirdly, without love, all our **faith** is **insufficient**. "If I have faith that can move mountains but have not love I am nothing" (1 Corinthians 13:2). It doesn't matter how strong our faith is if we don't have love. "The only thing that counts is faith expressing itself through love" (Galatians 5:6). Paul

> Without love, all our faith is insufficient, and all that we give is insignificant.

says, faith is important but without love, all our faith is insufficient.

Fourthly, without love, all that we **give** is **insignificant**. "If I give all I possess to the poor...but have not love, I gain nothing" (1 Corinthians 13:3). We can give everything we have, not just tithing, but much more than that. People can give with all kinds of motives. In the world some give for prestige, for recognition, for power, and to influence governments. Just because we give doesn't mean we love. We can give without loving but we cannot love without giving. Without love, all that we give is insignificant.

> To God, relationships are more important than achievements.

Fifthly, without love, all we **accomplish** is **inadequate**. "If I surrender my body to the flames," if we are burned alive for preaching the gospel, but don't have love for others, it is of no value whatsoever (1 Corinthians 13:3). We can rack up a list of impressive achievements and realize great accomplishments. We can build great organizations and sacrifice our lives for the greatest cause in the world. But, if we do not nurture and cultivate a spirit of love, we have missed what is most important in life. The point Paul makes is that to God, relationships are more important than achievements.

We can have the eloquence of an orator, the knowledge of a genius, the faith of a miracle worker, the generosity of a philanthropist, and the dedication of a martyr,[2] but the consistent practice of Christlike love with the people who know us, live and minister with us, is what demonstrates we are Christlike disciples. We must love other people like Jesus loves us. There is nothing more important in life than love. God is love. John doesn't say that "God has love." John says, "God is love" (1 John 4:16). In his presence we feel loved. This love is going to last for all eternity! Christlike love, God's perfect love, has been poured into our hearts by the Holy Spirit he has given us (Romans 5:5). What fuels our movement is having holy hearts filled with his perfect love.

"Dear friends, since God so loved us, we also ought to love one another. No one has ever seen God; but if we love one another, God lives in us and his love is made complete in us...we have confidence because in this world we are like him (1 John 4:11-12, 18). This is the message of our movement. God's love can totally fill our hearts! (Mark 12:28-31) This is what fuels us—the practice of God's love. We lead with love.

> This is the message of our movement. God's love can totally fill our hearts. This is what fuels us – the practice of God's love.

Questions for Reflection—Chapter 2

1. Why do you think Saul was such a zealous Christian killer? What do you think—was it his background, his personality, his beliefs, his spiritual training or a combination of these that made him so focused?

2. Saul was persecuting the church and trying to destroy the church. But the voice from heaven said to him, "I am Jesus whom you are persecuting." What does this tell us about the link between the imperfect, physical church and Jesus? Is this a new thought to you? Share your thoughts with the group.

3. Why do you think most people today find it much easier to love Jesus than to love his church? Does Jesus make a distinction between the two? What should our attitude toward the church be?

4. What characteristics did Barnabas have which made him so influential in the spiritual development of Paul?

5. In reading this chapter, was there anything you learned about Paul that you did not know before? If so, please share it with someone in your cohort, group or class.

6. How did walking and talking with Jesus over time change the message and attitudes of the apostle Paul? Can you identify in any way with this kind of journey in your own life? Why or why not?

7. The authors give five reasons why holy love is our main message. Which of these five has made the greatest impact in your life and thinking? How?

8. The authors state, "the consistent practice of Christlike love with the people who know us and live with us is what demonstrates we are a Christlike disciple. We must love other people like Jesus loves us. There is nothing more important in life than love!" What are your comments or reactions to this statement? Do you agree with it? Why or why not?

9. The authors state that "God's perfect love can be poured into our hearts by the Holy Spirit and that it is this love that fuels our movement." Do you agree with this statement? Why or why not?

10. How can you and your church better practice God's love? Is there anything you sense the Holy Spirit is whispering to you that you should change or do differently? If so, courageously share it with the members of your cohort, group or class.

3

Movements Focus on Outsiders

"Levi gave a large dinner at his home for Jesus. Everybody was there, tax men and other disreputable characters as guests at the dinner. The Pharisees and their religion scholars came to his disciples greatly offended. "What is he doing eating and drinking with crooks and 'sinners'?" Jesus heard about it and spoke up, "Who needs a doctor: the healthy or the sick? **I'm here inviting outsiders, not insiders**—an invitation to a changed life, changed inside and out."
(Luke 5:29-32, MSG).

Disciple-making is a journey of grace. Just like the activity of a Christian parent, intentional disciple-making does not begin at conversion, it begins at **conception.** Before a person comes to faith in Christ, prevenient grace[1] begins drawing them. **Saving grace** leads them into a grace-filled journey with Jesus, within the fellowship of his church. **Sanctifying grace** is both a divine moment and a process when a person fully embraces the agenda of Jesus and is entirely sanctified to God's will for their life. **Growth in grace** continues until they meet Jesus face to face.

> Disciple-making does not begin at conversion, it begins at conception. Before a person comes to faith in Christ, prevenient grace begins drawing them.

The disciple-making journey we take with Jesus is filled with grace. This journey does **not** begin at a person's conversion, it begins long before! When Paul had the vision of "**a man** from Macedonia,"

(Acts 16:10), God never intended the church's mission to be male centric. The first convert God was already preparing was **a woman** named Lydia who "the Lord opened her heart to respond to Paul's message" (Acts 16:14). Before Paul ever had the vision of the man from Macedonia, Lydia's **journey of grace** had already begun!

We find God's plan for the journey of grace throughout the Scriptures. "For the grace of God has appeared that offers salvation to **all people**" (Titus 2:11). The word grace (charis) appears in Luke, John, Acts, in Peter's writings and 100 times in the writings of Paul.[2] Beyond references to grace, there are also 158 references to favor in the scriptures, referencing both "favor with God" and "favor with people."[3] Grace is God's love and power in action in the life of every person. "God looks with favor on us in order that he may infuse us with his own moral energy...Grace is intended to change us; it does not leave us where we are."[4]

Here is just one story of tens of thousands of people who have been drawn to Jesus in this journey of grace. Chicago Central is one of 480+ districts from around the world that gather for an annual Assembly. Like most districts, the focus is on conversions, baptisms, new members, as well as membership and worship totals.

It is not uncommon for the Chicago Central District to celebrate 800-1,000 people every year who have begun this journey of grace. With 80+ churches cultivating a focus on outsiders, hundreds of people begin their grace journey and are baptized every year.

The superintendent, Larry McKain, has a personal friendship with one of these new believers within the church. He asked her to share her story with the District Assembly, from her perspective as a former outsider to the church. Her name is Tammie Selvey. She is a waitress at Bakers Square Restaurant in Bradley, Illinois. They first met when the Advisory Board Chair, Barry Huebner, and Larry would have breakfast. They would always sit at the same table, and she was usually their server. This is what Tammie shared at the Assembly.

"My name is Tammie Selvey and I am a new Christian. I never went to church as a child, except in the 5th grade, when we went to a Baptist church. We rode the bus. They would come and pick us up. My parents were divorced; my dad really didn't practice being a Christian. He and my step-mom sent us just so they could have a break on Sunday morning from us kids. That lasted for about a year.

> I think every Christian should always be reaching out to outsiders. Because they did, my life is changed.

"I had no church or God experience in high school. Glen and I were married when I was 21. He did have a church background; he would attend with his grandparents. We have four children, 3 girls and a boy. Life was very full. I always had to work on Sundays, so Glen watched the kids. God and Sunday church just didn't fit our schedule.

"Life got really hard when our son Justin got into trouble in high school. Alcohol was ruining his life. He was stealing and doing drugs. Our family was broken. The three girls didn't want to be around him. They stopped talking to him because of his bad influence and bad choices. All of this was going on in my life while I kept on working. I was a mess inside but not showing it. When Pastor Larry and Barry came in and asked how I was doing, I opened up. They prayed for me right there in the restaurant. That meant a lot to me.

"I think every Christian should always be reaching out to outsiders. Because they did, my life is changed. We should ask how people are doing. It didn't make me feel uncomfortable. It was a relief because I needed someone to talk to. Our family needed help.

"Justin became homeless. He finally came off the street and back to live with us and agreed to get help. I began taking him to Celebrate Recovery at the Gathering Point Church in Bourbonnais. There were so many days I would drive Justin to church but I wouldn't go in. I was afraid, but I watched Justin's life. The things I saw my son doing showed that he was a different person. I watched him change right before my eyes!

"I was really nervous because I didn't know anyone. But I finally thought, "I have to go in and see what is going on." So I got up the courage to walk into the church. It was not anything like what I expected. I sat through the service and I cried the whole time. Now I can actually make it through the service without crying. I began to take Sundays off from work just so I could attend church. That was a first! Now I love going. I feel like I can connect with the songs. Learning about God is very new to me, but the way Pastor Paul Johnson speaks, I feel like he is always talking right to me.

"Not only did I see a change in Justin, but I began to think, 'If God could forgive Justin, then maybe he could forgive me.' Also, when Justin went to church and Celebrate Recovery, I noticed that no one judged him. They made him feel welcomed, and I wanted that too.

"The church has brought our family back together. I work with Russell McDowell who also attends the church. He has become Justin's sponsor. We had tried to help Justin so many times on our own. We couldn't do it by ourselves. The church helped our son become sober again. I will never forget the day Justin shared his testimony with the church and got baptized.

"I'm so grateful for the church because I now have my son back! He is part of our family again. I want to thank Pastor Larry and Barry for praying for me. I want to also thank God for Russ and for the church caring for my family. And I'm grateful for all of you, for every church that is reaching out to outsiders, to people like me.

"I don't know a lot about the Bible. But I found this and texted it to Pastor Larry. "It's not how much Scripture you know, it's how much Scripture you live." I have gotten baptized at the church and am so glad to testify publicly about the change that Jesus has made in my life. Thank you all for caring!"

> "It's not how much Scripture you know, it's how much Scripture you live."

If your story is like Tammie's story, welcome to the Church of the Nazarene! Our church is designed with you in mind. We apologize when you first come into the church and we don't acknowledge there are first-time guests among us. We are sorry when we use terms we have not defined for you or we unintentionally act like we expect you to know as much as someone who has been in the church for a number of years. Our desire is to be a church with a focus on outsiders, filled with people on the grace journey together.

Thom Rainer gathered some main reasons why churches do not evangelize and focus on outsiders. Here are 12 of his results, organized into mistaken attitudes, beliefs, and behaviors. As you read these, prayerfully reflect on which ones may be temptations to you or your church.

Mistaken Attitudes

1. Some Christians have no sense of urgency to reach spiritually lost people.
2. Some Christians and church members are apathetic.
3. Some church members focus more on "getting my needs met" rather than reaching outsiders.

Mistaken Beliefs

4. Some churches have beliefs that focus more on what they are against than what they are for.

5. Some churches believe and use an ineffective strategy of "you come" rather than teaching Christians that "we go."

6. Some church members wrongly believe that evangelism is only the role of the pastor and paid church staff.

7. Some church members no longer believe Christ is the only way of salvation.

8. Some Christians no longer believe and share the truth of the gospel for fear they will offend others. In too many places, partisan thinking on political issues is replacing the gospel.

Mistaken Behaviors

9. Some churches are no longer "houses of prayer" being equipped to reach the lost.

10. Some Christians and church members do not befriend and spend time with outsiders.

11. Some church members are in "retreat mode" as the culture becomes more worldly and unbiblical.

12. Some churches have so many other activities that they are too busy to make evangelism and outsiders a priority.[5]

We are thankful that evangelism and reaching outsiders is a focus for Nazarenes throughout the world. As we study Nazarene churches that are healthy, growing, and multiplying throughout the world, **without exception** these churches focus on outsiders. They are not complicated churches. They thrive because they have common characteristics: 1) high expectations, 2) understanding spiritual realities, 3) being hospitable, 4) being guest friendly, 5) having outsider passion.

First, these are **high expectation** churches. These outsider focused churches believe God calls us to make a great Kingdom investment. These churches are convinced that deep within the heart of every
person is God's prevenient grace, drawing them and planting within them a desire to live a great life for God. Every person has a variety of talents and skills that gives them the capacity for greatness in the eyes of Jesus. These churches be-lieve every person has a desire to live **a great life**. No one lies awake at night dreaming and hoping that

> As we study Nazarene churches that are healthy, growing and multiplying throughout the world, without exception these are churches with a focus on outsiders.

at the end of their life they will reflect back on an average life that
inspired or blessed no one. No one wants to live a self-centered life.
The long-term result of that is misery. Churches that focus on outsiders
believe every person is created by God to be more than average!

They believe people are created to make a difference in the
world; created to live a life invested in a great Kingdom cause. We
never live a great life if we make a great investment in an average
cause. Churches that focus on outsiders challenge people to make a
great commitment, a great investment in a **great cause** — the agenda
of Jesus Christ! There is nothing on earth more important to which we
can give our lives.

Our world desperately needs to see and feel the love of "Christ
in action!" Our world is starving for Christians who will embrace the
agenda of Jesus and show Christ's love to all people. The church needs
Christians who see a need and do what they can to meet that need,
who bring hope where there is hurt, connection where there is isolation, comfort where there is fear, restoration where there is broken-

ness, friendship where there is loneliness, food where there is hunger, safety where there is danger, and shelter where there is homelessness.

> Being Christ in action should always occur before we open our mouths and talk about our faith in Jesus.

Being **Christ in action** should always occur **before** we open our mouths and talk about our faith in Jesus.

The goal of healthy, multiplying Nazarene churches is never to become a small church, intermediate church or large church. The goal is "to become all things to all people, so that by all possible means we might save **one more**" (1 Corinthians 9:22). This is the greatest cause a person can engage in, and it is worthy of our greatest investment!

These high expectation churches are **generous churches**. What is the opposite of generous? It is being selfish and stingy. Who struggles with less fear? Who has more joy? Who smiles more? Who has appreciative friends? Whose family is happier? Who has better emotional health? Whose life makes a greater impact—a selfish person or a generous person? Jesus taught that the key to life is to give your life away (Mark 8:35).

Generosity is one of the greatest legacies we can leave our family and our world. In our church we teach stewardship. This is an area in which every Christian can continue to grow. God's salvation is an expression of God's generosity (John 3:16). The church is an expression of God's generosity. Everything good in our lives is a result of God's generosity to us.

High expectation churches regularly ask people to invest and to participate. They challenge everyone to volunteer and find a place to serve. They never apologize for asking people to support the mission of the church with their time and money. Why? Because they so deeply believe that heaven will reveal the value of the church's mission.

These high expectation churches believe God calls every Christian to **live** the Great Commandment (Matthew 22:37-40) and **fulfill** the Great Commission (Matthew 28:18-20). We have seen hundreds of these churches (of all sizes) equipping people to make a great investment in a great cause. Every healthy, multiplying Nazarene church has this agenda of Jesus at its very core. This kind of church is **the hope of the world!**

> Healthy, multiplying churches that embrace the agenda of Jesus are the hope of the world!

We challenge every Christian in every Nazarene church on every district to listen to Jesus say again to you: "I tell you, open your eyes and look at the fields! They are ripe for harvest" (John 4:35). Every Nazarene church that goes through the challenges of adjusting their focus from only "insiders" to include "outsiders" embraces the agenda of Jesus. A church that exists only for insiders talks mainly about the privileges of membership. A church that includes outsiders talks about self-denial, sacrifice, and Kingdom expansion.

Adjusting the church's focus can be both expensive and uncomfortable. It is much easier and less stressful to exist only with an insider focus. But when a church has leaders willing to gracefully lead people toward becoming a high expectation church, leading them to make a great commitment and a great investment in a great cause, the agenda of Jesus thrives! Churches with an outsider focus are high expectation churches.

Secondly, these churches are very conscious of the **spiritual realities** involved in reaching outsiders. As they read the Scriptures, they know Jesus never played it safe and neither can they. Because they embrace the agenda of Jesus, they get close to the battle line no matter how difficult or dangerous the battle may get. When churches have only an insider focus, they bicker about a lot of things that do not matter, which leads to both temptation and sin within the church.

In the Old Testament, King David stayed home in the spring, at a time when all kings went off to war (2 Samuel 11:1). We don't know why David chose to stay home that particular spring, but it was during that time he had an affair with the wife of his neighbor and one of his most loyal soldiers who was out fighting on David's behalf. To cover up his sin, after David discovered the woman was pregnant, he had Uriah murdered (2 Samuel 11:2-27). Because David wasn't doing what he should have been doing, staying focused on the right issues, he opened himself to temptation and sin. If we don't pay attention to the true spiritual realities the church faces, temptation and sin will always emerge.

> Healthy churches give up a "nice, cleaned-up, perfect church" image and replace it with a "messy church" culture that stays in the trenches with real-world people who have real-world problems.

Churches that embrace these spiritual realities discover they must give up a "nice, cleaned-up, perfect church" image and replace it with a "messy church" culture that stays in the trenches with real-world people who have real-world problems. Only a divine moment from God can solve these problems! The greatest battles we face in every community are spiritual battles (Ephesians 6:10-12). Spiritual forces of evil still have too much influence, and when we zoom in from the big picture, Satan seems to win too many battles. Read the news from any day of the week, and you will see that Satan is having a heyday in our culture destroying many lives.

Satan, also known as the devil, is real. He is a fallen angel who rebelled against God. "The New Testament provides warrant for identifying the serpent of Genesis 3:1 with Satan (John 8:44; 2 Corinthians 11:3, 14; Revelation 12:9; 20:2).[6] He is called the prince of darkness and he exists. He is a thief who comes to steal, kill, and destroy (John 10:10). "God anointed Jesus of Nazareth with the Holy Spirit and power...he went around doing good and **healing all who were under the power of the devil**, because God was with him" (Acts 10:38). Through the life and death of Jesus, "the prince of this world has been driven out" (John 12:31).

The apostle Paul clearly understood these spiritual realities and wrote, "having disarmed the powers and authorities, Jesus made a public spectacle of them, triumphing over them by the cross" (Colossians 2:15). "For God has rescued us from the dominion of darkness and brought us into the kingdom of the Son he loves" (Colossians 1:13). Scripture abounds with references to "spiritual weapons that have divine power to demolish strongholds" and to "take captive people's thoughts to make them obedient to Christ" (2 Corinthians 10:4-5). These outsider focused churches are keenly aware of these **spiritual realities** all the time.

Thirdly, these outsider focused churches are **hospitable**. They make space for everyone. It doesn't take long after people are welcomed that they are invited to get involved. In many insider focused churches, people have to believe and behave before they can belong. In these outsider focused churches, the philosophy of being hospitable changes this old thinking. Instead, people are welcomed to immediately belong even before they believe and begin to behave like Christians.

Creating a climate of belonging does not require a church to change its theology or beliefs. Being hospitable simply means we allow everyone to begin their spiritual journey among us, regardless of whether or not they believe or behave as a Christian. Following the agenda and ministry of Jesus, we welcome people where they are and allow them time to make the journey toward becoming who Jesus desires them to be.

> Creating a climate of belonging does not require a church to change its theology or beliefs. It means we allow everyone to begin their spiritual journey among us, regardless of whether or not they believe or behave as a Christian.

Being hospitable always leads to great diversity and becoming a diverse church requires intentionality. Our vision of a **diverse** church comes from heaven: "After this I looked, and there before me was a great multitude that no one could count, from **every nation, tribe, people** and **language**, standing before the throne and before the Lamb" (Revelation 7:9). This is why we want the Nazarene church to be the most diverse church in town—diversity in ethnicity, color, educational background, political affiliation, careers, ages, social status, clothing style, hair color, even diversity in our favorite football, baseball, and soccer teams!

We believe there is something we can learn from every person who is different from us. Jesus taught, "I have **other sheep** that are not of this sheep pen. I must bring them also. They too will listen to my voice, and there shall be one flock and one shepherd" (John10:16). When the church becomes diverse, it can be messy. But it is beautiful when the church matures enough to appreciate, love and respect **everyone** who is **different.** Our church teaches us to "fix our eyes on Jesus, the pioneer and perfecter of our faith" (Hebrews 12:2). We are all an unfinished product of grace—we stay close to Jesus "so we do not grow weary and lose heart" (Hebrews 12:3).

These hospitable churches are usually led by pastors who keep the church simple so everyone can understand the purpose of the church and **get involved** in it. Churches with a focus on outsiders train their members not to be **missing in action** but to be **Christ in action!**

> When the church becomes diverse, it can be messy. But it is beautiful when the church matures enough to appreciate, love and respect everyone who is different.

People who are Christ in action serve their families, their parents, their church, their community and the world. They design their lives and schedules to go out and **DO SOMETHING** for the people around them. They have chosen NOT to be takers, but to be givers. As they study the Bible, they learn that Jesus gave us everything, so this is why we **freely give** (Matthew 10:8). Christians who are Christ in action find multiple ways to serve both inside and outside the church. In every attitude and action, they are **hospitable**.

Fourthly, these outsider focused churches are **guest-friendly.** A Scripture every one of these churches uses is Luke 5:31-32. Jesus responded to the Pharisees, "Who needs a doctor: the healthy or the sick? **I'm here inviting outsiders, not insiders**—an invitation to a changed life, changed inside and out." At some point in their lives, most people know what it feels like to be an outsider. For some it is relational, for others it is spiritual, for others it is educational or economic—there are many reasons. But most of us have had days when we felt this way. Wealthy business owners can be very lonely people, feeling like they will only be loved if they perform. Beautiful or handsome people in the world's eyes struggle with insecurity and isolation, feeling like they don't fit in.

There always comes a time for successful athletes when the

cheering and desire people have for them stops. They then can struggle with loneliness, self-doubt, and isolation. The handicapped, the poor, the marginalized, those who feel they are social misfits; all of these can also struggle with isolation. In the midst of this sea of human need to belong and believe, Jesus comes seeking to connect people and put them in a spiritual community where they can heal. Satan always comes seeking to separate and isolate people so he can steal, kill, and destroy them (John 10:10).

> In the midst of this sea of human need to belong and believe, Jesus comes seeking to connect people and put them in a spiritual community where they can heal.

Some of our churches are located in countries where members own cars. In these countries, churches with an outsider focus save their best parking spots for guests and those who are new. Their volunteers sacrifice by parking further away from the church building. They do not pray for easier lives, but instead that God will bless them as they serve with joy and are Christ in action.

These guest-friendly churches follow the example of Jesus and seek to keep the church simple. Jesus took a very complicated Old Testament system and made it simple: "Love God and love people" (Mark 12:28-31). Some churches, many times unknowingly, make it difficult for people to belong and complicated for people to believe. Guest-friendly churches stay simple. Simple does not mean simplistic. It is much harder to make things simple than it is to confuse people.

Guest-friendly churches offer simple messages that apply the Bible to people's everyday lives. They strive to balance grace and truth (John 1:14), and to help people live obedient to Jesus. These churches offer a simple plan for growing and maturing as a Christian. They build simple disciple-making systems and use simple structures.[7] They remove complexity so they can join the ranks of churches that become healthy with a plan to multiply.

> Guest-friendly churches stay simple. Simple does not mean simplistic. It is much harder to make things simple than it is to confuse people.

In Book 2 of the **MULTIPLYNAZ** series, we will talk about how new people coming into the church need a disciple-making pathway to take "next steps." Many churches emphasize the practice of the following five habits as their disciple-making path: 1) **attend worship** (and profess faith through baptism), 2) **serve** (volunteer and become involved in the ministry of the church), 3) **grow** in a small group, 4) regularly **give**, and 5) **invite** others. Some aspect of this simple path is talked about every week in every sermon. Every Sunday in these outsider focused churches, people are encouraged to take their next step of disciple-making.

What happens when the outsider focus of the church begins to fade? The following story illustrates this; a Nazarene pastor's millennial son was stationed in another state away from home. He texted his dad and asked for a recommendation for a church he could attend. His dad responded with a suggestion but was curious what his son experienced when he visited the church. The son shared the following report:

"Dad, everyone seemed to stare at me because they saw someone in their church with a tattoo. The service was 1 hour and 45 minutes long, and I'm sorry to say this, but it was boring. I couldn't wait to get out of there. Honestly, I felt like the pastor was winging the whole thing. I hope I am not being too critical. My perception was that it is a church where people demonstrate how spiritual they are, but not a church welcoming outsiders. As a newcomer, I was turned off." And then the son said this: "If I wasn't a Christian, I wouldn't go back to any church after visiting that church. I definitely wouldn't invite my friends who aren't Christians to come with me."

What would an outsider say who visited your church next week? Would they feel your church is guest-friendly? Churches that have learned to think differently about their guests know they are not the first church that has needed to make changes. In the New Testa-

> In outsider-focused churches, some aspect of the disciple-making path is talked about in every sermon. Every Sunday, people are encouraged to take their next step of disciple-making.

ment, the early church took the mission of Jesus very seriously and both Jews and Gentiles started to turn to Jesus and join the church.

All these new outsiders caused church leaders to gather in Jerusalem to discuss the big issue that was dividing them. Some Jewish believers thought it was great that Gentiles were now believers in Christ, but thought it was important for these new Gentile followers to be circumcised. What a membership requirement! After lots of discussion, James, the head of the church in Jerusalem, offered these thoughts:

"It is my judgment, therefore, that **we should not make it difficult for the Gentiles who are turning to God**. Instead we should write to them, telling them to abstain from food polluted by idols, from sexual immorality, from the meat of strangled animals and from blood. For the law of Moses has been preached in every city from the earliest times and is read in the synagogues on every Sabbath" (Acts 15:19-21). Does your church discuss how to include outsiders? How to prepare for them? How to pray for them? How to expect them? These are important questions. If God has to choose a church to connect with a seeker, he will choose one that has been preparing to receive that person. In guest-friendly churches, church volunteers pray, plan, and work to make it possible for new people to experience a "divine moment" and turn to God. Volunteers who love, pray, give and serve make it possible for outsiders to come back home to God.

Every week it takes hundreds of thousands of Nazarene volunteers in tens of thousands of churches worldwide to help our movement keep its focus on outsiders. Our churches are encouraged to be **guest-friendly** because what is at stake is the mission of Jesus to save every person in the world (John 3:16)!

Fifthly, these outsider focused churches have high levels of **outsider passion.** Paul writes, "Though I am free and belong to no one, I have made myself a slave to everyone, to win as many as possible. To the Jews I became like a Jew, to win the Jews. To those under the law I became like one under the law...so as to win those under the law. To those not having the law I became like one not having the law...so as to win those not having the law. To the weak I became weak, to win the weak. I have become all things to all people so that by all possible means I might save some. I do all this for the sake of the gospel, that I may share in its blessings" (1 Corinthians 9:19-23).

We become all things to all people so that by all possible means we might save **one more person** (1 Corinthians 9:22). Jesus taught that the spiritual life of one person is worth more than the whole world (Mark 8:36-37). The mission of churches with an outsider focus is to go after that one lost person, just like Jesus does, until we find them (Luke 15:4).

Churches with an outsider passion don't mind being **dangerous churches.** The early church was under severe persecution and Paul was traveling and teaching everyone he could about Jesus. When he told people he was going up to Jerusalem, they pleaded with him not to go because they feared he would be killed. Here is Paul's response: "Why are you weeping and breaking my heart? I am ready not only to be bound, but also to die in Jerusalem for the name of the Lord Jesus." When he would not be dissuaded, we gave up and said, "The Lord's will be done" (Acts 21:13-14).

Paul accepted the dangerous mission God gave him. His call was to be all things to all people so that by all possible means he might save one more person. This is a dangerous prayer: "Lord, I am ready to die for you, to accomplish your mission." In the USA/Canada region, for the most part, we do not experience danger as we serve Christ. In many other parts of the world, this is not the case.

Paul went to Jerusalem, encouraging fellow believers and helping them grow in Christ. "When the seven days were nearly over, some Jews from the province of Asia saw Paul at the temple. They stirred up the whole crowd…The whole city was aroused, and the people came running from all directions. **Seizing Paul**, they **dragged him** from the temple, and immediately the gates were shut. While they were **trying to kill him,** news reached the commander of the Roman troops that the whole city of Jerusalem was in an uproar. He at once took some officers and soldiers and ran down to the crowd. When the rioters saw the commander and his soldiers, they **stopped beating Paul**" (Acts 21:27, 30-32).

Paul was arrested and rather than complaining how unfair this was, he used the opportunity to share his faith with the whole crowd! (Acts 22:1-22) The next day Paul stood before the chief priests and all the members of the Sanhedrin, sharing his story of faith in Christ, and a dispute broke out. "The commander was afraid Paul **would be torn to pieces** by them" (Acts 23:10). While still in jail, there was a plot to **kill Paul,** so they transferred him to Caesarea (Acts 23:12-35). Paul was falsely imprisoned for two years and then brought before Festus and King Agrippa and he did the same thing each time—he shared his story about coming to faith in Jesus!

As Paul was sharing his life-changing story about first persecuting Christians, then meeting Jesus and doing a 180-degree turnaround, "Agrippa said to Paul, "Do you think that in such a short time you can persuade me to be a Christian?" Paul replied, "Short time or long—I pray to God that not only you but all who are listening to me today may become what I am, except for these chains" (Acts 26:28-29).

Churches with a high level of **outsider passion** have this same spirit—they want to help outsiders connect with Christ and a church family. They want to love people and help them become who God created them to be. Some will come to faith quickly; others may take years. But **no one is too far away**. One at a time, people all over the world are finding salvation and hope in Jesus through these churches with high levels of outsider passion!

> Some will come to faith quickly; others may take years. **But no one is too far away.**

• Can you imagine a church where every person is committed to building authentic relationships, where everyone's spiritual journey is honored, and freedom is given to take steps toward Jesus at their own pace?

• Can you imagine a church where there are no outsiders or insiders but where EVERYONE is welcomed into a worship service, valued and invited to belong?

- Can you imagine a church where everyone works hard to keep things simple and keep the main thing front and center?

- Can you imagine a church where there are no walls, no masks, no taboo subjects, where every member loves as Jesus loves and is willing to lay down their life even for those who may have hurt them? (Matthew 5:43-44)

- Can you imagine a church where the one who is struggling with sexual sin, pornography, a prior abortion, the one who struggles with going to strip clubs when out of town, the one who was sexually abused as a child and doesn't know how to relate to men, the one who had an alcoholic parent and has become a workaholic, and the one who stole property from his mom and dad to finance a meth addiction—can you imagine a church where **all are welcome** to begin the journey of grace, where they hear and understand truth from God's Word and where they respond and find hope and healing in Jesus?

> Can you imagine a church where **all are welcome** to begin the journey of grace, where they hear and understand truth from God's Word and where they respond and find hope and healing in Jesus?

- Can you imagine a church where acts of kindness with no strings attached are the norm and people look forward to being asked to give financially—where weekly offerings are used to help people physically and spiritually in their local church and around the world?[8]

Deep within our souls the Holy Spirit keeps fueling our commitment to continual movement forward, reminding us that we MUST start more churches like this. We must revitalize existing churches to operate like this. We need EVERY church to practice **disciple-making as a journey of grace** and focus on outsiders![9]

Questions for Reflection —Chapter 3

1. The authors state, "Just like the activity of a Christian parent, intentional disciple-making does not begin at conversion, it begins at conception. Before a person comes to faith in Christ, prevenient grace begins drawing them." Do you agree that God begins working in a person's life long before they experience God's saving grace? Why or why not?

2. What does the phrase "favor with God" mean to you? What does "favor with people" mean to you? In your opinion, what does this look like when it happens in a person's life?

3. Do you believe it is possible for a church to experience and enjoy the "favor of God?" Why or why not? If so, what do you think this would look like?

4. What was your reaction to the testimony of Tammie Selvey? What lessons did you learn? Does your church have anyone who has had a spiritual journey similar to Tammie? Who?

5. How does your church celebrate spiritual change in a person's life? Does your church give people the opportunity to share their testimony with the congregation? How is this done?

6. How can congregations do a better job of welcoming people like Tammie into the church?

7. Slowly and out loud, read the wrong attitudes, wrong beliefs and wrong behaviors of some churches and Christians (listed on pages 59-60). Which ones stand out to you? Which ones are temptations in your church? In your personal life? Talking only about yourself, not the church, courageously share with the members of your cohort, group or class.

8. Reflect on the characteristics of healthy, multiplying churches. What did you learn in reading about these churches? Which of these were new to you? Share which of the five you feel your church should begin developing first to move forward.

9. What can churches do to overcome the temptation to talk only about membership "privileges?" How can we better develop a culture which embraces self-denial and sacrifice? Do you believe the Bible teaches that we should embrace these?

10. The Bible makes clear there are spiritual realities which include spiritual warfare. What did you learn from this part of the chapter? What practical steps can you take to apply them in your church? In your personal life?

11. In outsider focused churches, people are welcomed to belong before they believe and behave as a Christian. How does your church do at welcoming non-Christians who are just beginning their spiritual journey? How can you improve?

12. Discuss the differences between a philosophy of believe-behave-belong and a philosophy of belong-believe-behave. How can your church change its way of thinking without changing its theology or beliefs?

13. How diverse is your congregation? Ethnicity? Color? Educational backgrounds? Political affiliations? Careers? Ages? Social status? Clothing style? Sports teams? How open are people in your church to listen and learn from people who are very different from them?

14. How often does your church explain disciple-making next steps to attenders and guests? How simple and understandable are these steps to take?

15. After reading the section on "outsider passion," on a scale of 1 to 10, 1 being very low outsider passion and 10 incredibly high outsider passion, how would you rate yourself? How would you rate your church? Ask your group, cohort or class to pray for you that your passion level would move up at least 1 or 2 points in the days ahead.

4

What We Believe About the Church

"Christ loved the church and gave himself up for her to make her holy, cleansing her by the washing with water through the Word, and to present her to himself as a radiant church, without stain or wrinkle or any other blemish, but holy and blameless." (Ephesians 5:25-27)

How we think makes a big difference. It makes all the difference in the world and in the world to come. How we think is not so much what we say, but really shows more who we are. What we ultimately become is determined by how we think. There is a saying based on Galatians 6:7 about how we reap what we sow.

Sow a thought, reap an act. Sow an act, reap a habit.

Sow a habit, reap a character. Sow a character, reap a destiny.

How we think leads to how we act. How we act determines the habits we form. The habits we form determine the character we possess. Our character determines our destiny. This is not only true of individuals; this is true of local churches and districts. This is true of fields, universities, and regions.

> What we ultimately become is determined by how we think. This is true of local churches, districts, fields, universities and regions.

In Book 2 of the **MULTIPLYNAZ** series, we will look at how the spiritual habits we develop impact the "soil" of the church (Mark 4:28). Contagious churches teach disciple-making habits to their people that cause spiritual "seed" to easily grow. Their actions and habits create the character of a contagious church. The formation of a church's character and culture flows from a church's thinking. This is why the way we think is so important. In our local church, we are a product of how we think.

If our movement is to be all God has dreamed for it to be, it will begin with us and the way we think. If we are to be used in our generation to help the church be what Jesus envisioned her to become, we must seek to think the way Jesus thinks. We must see lost people (outsiders) the way Jesus sees lost people (Luke 15:1-32). We must act the way Jesus would act if he were leading the church in our skin...be-cause he is! We are his body, his flesh in the world today (1 Corinthians 12:27). As his church, we are given the incredible promise that it is possible for us to have "the mind of Christ" (1 Corinthians 2:16). Jesus thinks about his Bride all the time!

> We must act the way Jesus would act if he were leading the church in our skin...because he is!

We have all been to weddings. The first miracle Jesus performed was at a wedding (John 2:1-11). In the Old Testament, God refers to the people of Israel as his Bride (Hosea 2:19-20). In the New Testament, Paul likens the nature of the church to the marriage of a husband and wife: "the two will become one flesh. This is a profound mystery—but I am talking about Christ and the church" (Ephesians 5:32). In the final book of the Bible, John describes the greatest wedding of all that will take place at the Marriage Supper of the Lamb (Revelation 19:6-9). The church is the Bride of Christ and will belong to him for all eternity.

Our Doctrine of the Church

In our Articles of Faith, Manual paragraph 11 explains our doctrine of the church. "We believe in the Church, the community that confesses Jesus Christ as Lord, the covenant people of God made new in Christ, the Body of Christ called together by the Holy Spirit through the Word...The mission of the Church in the world is to share in the redemptive and reconciling ministry of Christ in the power of the Spirit."[1] The next part of our Manual paragraph is very important theologically because it shapes our understanding of how the church may look in different settings and contexts, both locally and globally. Our Article of Faith states, "The church is a historical reality that organizes itself in **culturally conditioned forms...**"

We have culturally conditioned forms of church both in the USA/Canada Region and beyond. Many people living in the United States have a certain culturally conditioned form of church they like. This is good, very good!

> "The church is a historical reality that organizes itself in **culturally conditioned forms...**"

We need dozens and dozens of the kind of church you envision when we use the word "church." Every person, every pastor, every leader has a preference for their "culturally conditioned form" of church. We hope you don't lose it. Please keep it and help us multiply it. In our polity, Superintendents are given the responsibility to help every congregation within their district become a healthy, multiplying church.

The Board of General Superintendents has wisely defined a church as "any group that meets regularly for spiritual nurture, worship, or instruction...with an identified leader and is aligned with the message and mission of the Church..."[2] Four key things are found in this statement: 1) **worship**, 2) **community**, 3) **accountability**, and 4) **mission**.

Notice here, the church does not require a building or property. It does not have to have a clergy pastor. It can be led by a lay pastor who is provided theological education. A "church" is not required to be a certain size. It does not have to worship on Sunday. It can worship on other days of the week.

> A church is "any group that meets regularly for spiritual nurture, worship, or instruction… with an identified leader and is aligned with the message and mission of the Church."

Paul says in Romans 14:5, "One person considers one day more sacred than another, another person considers every day alike. Each one should be fully convinced in his own mind." Here Paul gives us permission to worship and lead people to Christ every day of the week, not just on Sunday![3]

The church has never had to be a certain size to be an effective church. It can even be a "micro-church" (churches in homes). If we are to reach every community and cultural group on every district, we must begin thinking differently. We should embrace missionary thinking and missionary strategies as we enter a secular culture. Every church in the world usually begins small. We encourage the planting of hundreds of micro-churches in unreached neighborhoods throughout the world. In the megacities of the world where real estate is cost prohibitive, micro-churches will no doubt be a key way the church continues its exponential expansion.

This multiplication of the church is embedded in our doctrine of the church. The church always exists "in culturally conditioned forms." We need dozens of new kinds of churches in different cultural forms.[4] It takes all kinds of churches in all kinds of places to reach all kinds of people. The churches of the future will not just be Anglo churches, Black churches or Hispanic churches. Many will be multi-cultural as a reflection of their community. To achieve her global mission, the church will have to create a multitude of new kinds of churches within our districts all over the world. We are grateful for the tens of thousands of mature church leaders who will **embrace these new churches** and **their leaders**!

> A "church" does not require a building or property. It does not have to have a clergy pastor. It can be led by a lay pastor.

As the world continues to change, so must the church. NEVER our message, but our methods, style and strategies must always keep changing. We must keep adjusting and innovating if we are to penetrate every sub-culture and micro-context on our districts with the gospel of Jesus Christ.

Our Church Minimums

The Greek word for church is "ecclesia." The study of the church is called ecclesiology. When we talk about our church (or ecclesial) minimums, we mean, "What are the church minimums that must be present for a group of people coming together to be considered "a church?" In everything we do, our church must be biblical and simple, just like the early church. As Nazarenes, we affirm micro-churches as the most basic expression of the church. When two or three believers come together in Christ's name, Jesus is present (Matthew 18:20). If these believers choose to work together in authentic worship, genuine community, being accountable and aligned with the mission of Jesus to share the gospel and expand the "ecclesia," they are the church! So, for us 1) **worship,** 2) **community,** 3) **accountability,** and 4) **mission** are our church minimums.

> We must keep adjusting and innovating if we are to penetrate every sub-culture and micro-context on our districts with the gospel of Jesus Christ.

As Nazarenes, we always seek to empower rather than control. We believe starting new churches is the most effective method of evangelism and a Nazarene essential to making Christlike disciples in the nations.[5] We encourage all of our churches to mother new churches and all new churches to have a mother church. When this is not possible, the church planter becomes directly accountable to the District Superintendent. We can start a church anywhere God raises up a leader and there are lost people who need the gospel.

What Jesus Believes About the Church

The mission of the church is "to make Christlike disciples in the nations." Christlikeness is the standard by which we measure "every thought to make it obedient to Christ" (2 Corinthians 10:5). "Jesus left us an example, that we should follow in his steps" (1 Peter 2:21). Our call as church leaders is to teach our generation to follow Jesus by giving themselves up for the imperfect group of people Jesus gave himself up for—the church. Although Jesus and God are both perfect, the church, the physical expression of Jesus in the world today, is not perfect. This is not a surprise or a discouragement to God.

Jesus knew his church would be imperfect when he planted the very first one in Jerusalem. If you feel that you have problems with your church, look at the problems Jesus dealt with in his church.

> For us, 1) **worship**, 2) **community**, 3) **accountability** and 4) **mission** are our church minimums.

1. The treasurer was stealing money from him. (John 12:6)
2. One of his key church leaders betrayed him. (Luke 22:47-48)
3. When he needed his leadership team, they slept. (Matt 26:40)
4. When pressured, the leadership team deserted him.(Matt 26:55-56)
5. His closest key leader disowned him. (Matt 26:75)

Several encouraging truths stand out as we evaluate the problems in the church with which Jesus worked. If your treasurer is not stealing from you, if you are not being betrayed by key leaders, if only half of your leadership team sleeps during meetings, if all your leaders are not deserting you and if your best supporter has not disowned you, you are doing better than Jesus did.

If you have seen any movie about the life and death of Jesus, replay the scenes in your mind. The treasurer is stealing money, key leaders are betraying Jesus, and his leadership team cannot stay awake. When his key leaders do wake up, they desert him, and his closest supporter denies knowing him with a string of curses. Here is the question. Would you go to the cross for that group of people? Would you give yourself up in sacrifice for this kind of imperfect church? Jesus did.

If these things happened to Jesus as our leader, we can certainly expect there will be many kinds of problems every church leader will have. Just like we do, Jesus worked with a group of very imperfect people. He loved the church and gave himself up for her (Ephesians 5:25). When we follow his example and love the church, we are loving the institution God has chosen to bring salvation to the world and the vehicle he is using to prepare us to meet him. Jesus loved the church and believed it was the hope of the world! He knew the only way local congregations would become healthy, multiplying churches all over the world is for people to follow his example and give themselves up for the church and its mission.

> When we love the church, we are loving the institution God has chosen to bring salvation to the world and the vehicle he is using to prepare us to meet him.

Agenda Harmony with Jesus

Jesus changed the world with shared thoughts and inspired ideas. Through the power of the Holy Spirit, the movement of Christianity erupted, and that movement has launched the Church of the Nazarene into the 21st century. Jesus has a vision for his church. He gave himself up for the church and what she could be. He changed the world with teaching—with thoughts and ideas that came from God. He said, "For I did not speak of my own accord, but the Father who sent me commanded me what to say and how to say it" (John 12:49).

We can never underestimate the power of God-inspired thoughts and ideas. This is why the teaching and preaching that occurs in our churches every week has so much potential! God uses it to literally transform people's lives. Jesus died for each and every church. He carries your church in his heart and mind. He says to us, "I know your deeds, your love and faith, your service and perseverance" (Revelation 2:19). Jesus has called us to join with him as he builds his church (Matthew 16:18). We become more effective as we stay "connected to the vine" (John 15:1-2), learning to speak beyond our own ideas. We must sense what the Father and the Spirit are whispering to us (1 Kings 19:12, Isaiah 30:21, John 10:27). Listening to Jesus, we must learn what to say and how to say it to the church we love and serve.

We need his Word and his Spirit instructing (John 14:26) and cleansing us (John 15:3). Great agenda harmony is fueled the more we move beyond strategy and truly embrace what we believe: "the Body of Christ called together by the Holy Spirit **through the Word**."[6] We can all testify when we face obstacles that

> We can never underestimate the power of God-inspired thoughts and ideas.

cause us to stay dependent (John 15:5), it is the power of Scripture that changes our way of thinking (Jeremiah 20:9, 23:29). We want to have the mind of Christ (1 Corinthians 2:16). As he keeps shaping us, he fuels our spirits with a passion for Christlikeness. This causes us to continually seek agenda harmony with him.

The more we embrace the church's mission "to make Christlike disciples in the nations," the more we learn to follow Jesus' agenda. This fuels questions like, "What does Jesus think about this?" "How does he feel?" "What would Jesus do?" We find ourselves praying prayers like, "Lord, help me to cry over the things which make you cry, to laugh at the things which make you laugh, to have a heart for the things for which you have a heart."

We grow deeper in our desire to think the way Jesus thinks and to feel what he feels. We want our will to be guided by his will and our values to reflect his values. We want our spirits to be filled with his Spirit and our hearts to be aligned with his heart. We want to learn how to think the way Jesus thinks. We want his agenda for our church to be our agenda. As sanctified followers of Jesus, this leads us to live with a spirit of repentance.[7]

The Greek word for repent, that describes the cultivation of this kind of sanctified heart is "metanoia," which means "a change of mind and a corresponding change of life." The Spirit that fills our spirit and calls the church together keeps drawing us to the Word. We wish every decision we make once we choose to align with the agenda of Jesus, consistently lives up to the ideals of the paragraphs above. It does not, but we can have "purity of intention."[8]

> We want to think the way Jesus thinks and feel what he feels. We want our will to be guided by his will and our values to reflect his values.

Over time we feel our minds slowly being renewed. More and more we are less driven by what we think and more consistently guided by what Jesus thinks.

Gaining agenda harmony with Jesus is a process. Paul describes it this way: "Do not conform any longer to the pattern of this world but be transformed by the renewing of your mind. Then you will be able to test and approve what God's will is—his good, pleasing and perfect will" (Romans 12:2).

If the church we serve is to achieve the mission of Jesus, to "go and make disciples of all nations, baptizing them and teaching them to obey everything I have commanded you" (Matthew 28:19), it will begin with our commitment to humbly keep changing the way we think. It will require us to let God regularly renew our minds by his Word so we gain his agenda and come into harmony

> If your heart is responsive, the movement has already begun where you live.

with the other church leaders with whom we serve. The result will be locking arms together to create the vision Jesus has for his church, being "like-minded, having the same love, being one in spirit and one in purpose" (Philippians 2:2). Can you imagine a local church where every member chooses to think like Jesus thinks and seeks his agenda above all else? Can you imagine a global movement of believers who have embraced the agenda of Jesus and want his will above everything else? Do you have an interest in being part of a movement of God like this? If your heart is responsive, the movement has already begun where you live!

Questions for Reflection—Chapter 4

1. Do you agree with the statements that our thoughts impact our actions? That our actions shape our habits? That our habits shape our character? Discuss this in your group. Can you give an example of this in your own life?

2. Reflect on this statement: "We must act the way Jesus would act if he were leading the church in our skin...because he is!" If Jesus were the leader of your church, is there anything he would do differently? If so, what?

3. "The church is a historical reality that organizes itself in **culturally conditioned forms...**" Can you think of examples of the way churches are different in various parts of the world? How are they different in different cultures? Can churches be very different in the same town? Why?

4. Should churches all be the same within a district? Or should they be very diverse? Why or why not? If we have many different kinds of churches within a district, how will that change us?

5. Does a church have to have a building? Does it have to have an ordained pastor? Does it need to be a certain size? Does it have to worship on Sunday? Why?

6. When a church has people who begin to think like missionaries all the time, how does that change the way a church operates?

7. Can the methods, styles, and strategies of the church change and the church still be the church? How does continual change help the church penetrate "every sub-culture and micro-context" of our district? What could that look like?

8. Discuss the four "church minimums" the church uses around the world. Do you agree with these? Are you tempted to "add" anything to them? Why or why not?

9. Discuss the imperfect church that Jesus started. How does this make you feel about your imperfect church?

10. Why is Jesus willing to "give himself up," to sacrifice his life for such an imperfect group of people? Are you willing to do the same for your church? Discuss how committed Jesus is to us. Pause and pray that the commitment level in your church will rise.

11. Do you live with a "spirit of repentance" like the authors describe? How can you gain better agenda harmony with Jesus? How does Jesus want to keep changing the way you think? Share this with your group. Ask them to pray for you that you would stay open to being changed by Jesus.

5
Why Nazarenes Practice "Interdependence"

> "We now realize how true it is that God does not show favoritism but accepts people from **every nation** who fear him
> and do what is right." (Acts 10:34-35)

What a marvelous creation of God! What an incredible design! What a divine strategy! God takes imperfect people all over the world who believe in Jesus and he gathers them into divine groups. These groups meet regularly for worship, community, encouragement and service to others. They lock arms with each other to provide a witness to the world that they are one with Jesus and the Father (John 17:21-23).

In the Bible, the word church is used two ways. First, it is used to refer to every Christian who has ever lived in time. This is the church "universal," and the word church is used this way in the Bible four times. The other 110 times it is used in the Bible, the word church refers to a body of believers with whom we spiritually connect. The church at Corinth, the church at Philippi, the church at Thessalonica and hundreds more—these were all congregations in which individual Christians remained connected to one another.

In early church teaching, it was inconceivable that someone would claim to be a Christian and not be both connected to a local body of Christ and part of the global movement of God. Dozens of commands given to Christians in the New Testament cannot be obeyed unless a believer is both connected and active in a local church. There are dozens of "one anothers" in the New Testament, i.e. "love one another" (John 13:34), "be devoted to one another," "honor one another" (Romans 12:10), "live in harmony with one another" (Romans 12:16), "accept one another" (Romans 15:7), "serve one another" (Galatians 5:13), "instruct one another" (Romans 15:14), "carry each other's burdens" (Galatians 6:2), "be kind and compassionate to one another," "forgiving each other" (Ephesians 4:32), "submit to one another" (Ephesians 5:21), "encourage each other," "build each other up" (1 Thessalonians 5:11), "don't grumble against each other" (James 5:9), "confess your sins to each other," "pray for each other" (James 5:16), "offer hospitality to one another" (1 Peter 4:9), and "live in harmony with one another" (1 Peter 3:8), just to name a few!

> Throughout the book of Acts, the Holy Spirit leads the church to maintain connectedness with other local churches. The theological word for this is "interdependence."

Throughout the book of Acts, the Holy Spirit leads the church to maintain connectedness with other local churches. The theological word for this is "**interdependence**." The movement of God through the people of God required relationships to be established and maintained, especially where the church was expanding beyond the local level. The movement broke out in Samaria when Philip was sent there by the Spirit (Acts 8:5). The apostles in Jerusalem sent Peter and John to Samaria to help fuel the movement by leading them to understand and receive the Holy Spirit (Acts 8:14-15).

The movement spread to Africa when the Holy Spirit directed Philip to leave the revival in Samaria and meet the Ethiopian eunuch (Acts 8:26-39). The movement crossed all kinds of ethnic and cultural barriers when Peter embraced a Roman centurion and broke Jewish law to enter his house (Acts 10:27-28). Peter's vision led to the discovery that "God would accept people from **every nation** who fear him and do what is right" (Acts 10:35). The seeds of a global movement of God through the people of God exploded with new possibilities!

The movement was fueled by the Holy Spirit sending out Paul and Barnabas to Cyprus and then throughout what is today modern Turkey (Acts 13:1-14:28). This movement of God never developed a spirit of "independence" in the church's expansion. We see the early church always maintaining a spirit of interconnectedness and "**interdependence**."[1] This is why in the Church of the Nazarene we believe so strongly that our "interdependence" has New Testament roots.

> The movement of God through the people of God required relationships to be established and maintained, especially where the church was expanding beyond the local level.

When major questions arose about both doctrine and church operations, "Paul and Barnabas were appointed, along with some other believers, to go up to Jerusalem to see the apostles and elders" (Acts 15:2) to discuss the issues. Why? Because they were never independent but interdependent. "It seemed good to the Holy Spirit and to us" was the spirit with which the church operated (Acts 15:28).

Even when ministry differences became apparent and separation occurred between Paul and Barnabas (Acts 15:39), this did not hinder Paul's commitment to remain interdependent with the church. As he and Silas "traveled from town to town, they delivered the decisions reached by the **apostles and elders in Jerusalem** for the people to obey" (Acts 16:4). This caused the churches "to be strengthened in the faith and grow in numbers daily" (Acts 16:5). **The evidence for "interdepen-**

dence" in the early church between congregations is indisputable.
As the church organized itself into culturally conditioned forms (both
Jewish and Gentile churches), individual churches never sought to op-
erate independently from each other. Everyone operated with a deep belief in the interdependence of the church. The movement of God through the people of God was too valuable to allow the non-essentials within the movement to divide them.

> The evidence for "interdependence" in the early church between congregations is indisputable.

Following these examples in the New Testament, Nazarenes choose to operate interdependently with the local, district, and global church[2] for seven biblical reasons. First, **this is where we spiritually mature in Christlikeness.** Maturity cannot be achieved without community. The church is the institution God has chosen to prepare us to meet him and spend time with him for all eternity. The church is where we are regularly washed with the water of his Word and challenged to become more like him (Ephesians 5:26-27). We move to new levels of Christlikeness when we embrace our brothers and sisters from different communities, cultures, and countries.

Secondly, **the church is our spiritual family.** Paul writes, "Let us do good to all people, especially those who belong to the family of believers" (Galatians 6:10). Our spiritual family, the church, will last longer than even our physical family. In heaven, we will be in the family of the church forever. In the

> Our spiritual family is not just local, but district-wide and global. We can travel the world and instantly meet people who are part of our global family of believers.

Church of the Nazarene, our spiritual family is not just local, but district-wide and global. We can travel the world and instantly meet people who are part of our global family of believers.

Thirdly, **the church is where we discover and use our spiritual gifts.** Paul writes, "Now about spiritual gifts, brothers, I do not want you to be ignorant" (1 Corinthians 12:1). "Each one should use whatever gift he has received to serve others" (1 Peter 4:10). If we do not use our God-given spiritual gifts to help build up Christ's church, the church and the work of Jesus in the world will not be what it could be. Every part is essential as the church "grows and builds itself up in love" (Ephesians 4:16). All the spiritual gifts a local church needs, God can and will raise up within that church. Different gifts expressed through the different cultural forms of the church in different parts of the world make us better.

Fourthly, **the church is where we receive spiritual protection.** The Scriptures instruct pastors, "Guard...the flock of which the Holy Spirit has made you overseers. Be shepherds of the church of God... because savage wolves will come in among you...and distort the truth" (Acts 20:28-29). Part of the church's responsibility is to help people separate truth from error and provide spiritual protection.

Fifthly, **the church provides us with spiritual accountability through practicing interdependence.** The Bible says, "Brothers and sisters, if someone is caught in a sin, you who live by the Spirit should restore that person gently...Carry each other's burdens and in this way you will fulfill the law of Christ" (Galatians 6:1-2). An important benefit of church membership is accountability, which everyone needs for their spiritual growth.[3] This is a maturity issue as well as an issue of obedience to the teachings of Jesus (Matthew 28:19, John 14:23-24). Every member in the Church of the Nazarene is accountable to their local church. Every minister in the Church of the Nazarene is accountable to a district. Districts throughout the world are accountable to each other through the General Assembly.[4]

> Not only are pastors accountable to their churches and to superintendents, superintendents are accountable to pastors and to each other... The way we are accountable is one of our greatest strengths.

Every superintendent elected by the church, either by a District Assembly or General Assembly is accountable and interdependent, along with and **to every pastor.** Not only are pastors accountable to their churches and to superintendents, superintendents are accountable to pastors and to each other. This is the way a healthy, multiplying church movement should operate. The way we are accountable and interdependent with each other is one of the greatest strengths of the church!

Sixthly, **the church provides local churches the opportunity to do together what is impossible separately.** When local churches come together and lock arms, they are unstoppable. They relate with their community. They maintain connection and interdependence with churches on their district. They can learn from other churches within the Nazarene network in their region and beyond. Wherever a church is interdependent, healthy and multiplying, it is the result of local communities, churches and districts gaining agenda harmony to do together what we can never do by ourselves.

Lastly, **the church is created by the Holy Spirit to help us fulfill Christ's Great Commission.** Every Christian is called to "make disciples of all nations" (Matthew 28:19). Separate and isolated, we cannot become the locally and globally-minded Christians God wants us to be. It is by linking arms in local communities among churches and districts that we can make a huge impact locally and also send and support missionaries in 160+ countries of the world.

We are a multi-national church, with six regional offices located throughout the world. Most people have heard of Apple, Inc., a company that sells computers and phones, etc. It is one of the wealthiest and most well-known companies in the world and the first company in history to gain a market cap[5] of over $1 trillion. Apple's market cap makes the company larger than the GDP (Gross Domestic Product)[6] of 183 out of the 199 countries for which the World Bank[7] has GDP data. Apple, Inc., has a lot more money than the church, but only operates in 24 countries of the world (ones where they can make money). The Church of the Nazarene operates in 160+ countries, almost 7 times more than Apple. We do not enter countries based on economic factors. **We operate within the poorest countries of the world.** Our only agenda is the agenda of Jesus.

> Apple, Inc. only operates in 24 countries of the world. The Church of the Nazarene operates in 160+ countries, almost 7 times more countries than Apple.

Because we are a global movement of God, we now send missionaries from dozens of countries to the locations where they are most needed and suited. We are not limited to just a few countries or negatively impacted by what may be happening in the geo-political realm. **Every country has an equal place at the Nazarene global movement table.** No country is deemed more important than any other. The Church of the Nazarene is a 21st century expression of the vision given to Peter by God. "God does not show favoritism but accepts people

Every country has an equal place at the Nazarene global movement table. No country is deemed more important than any other.

from **every nation** who fear him and do what is right" (Acts 10:34-35). What a privilege to participate in this kind of an international, interdependent movement of God through the people of God!

Questions for Reflection—Chapter 5

1. Discuss the "one anothers" that are listed in the New Testament. How are they currently practiced in your church? Take a moment and thank God for the way your church is becoming more like the early church. What practical steps can you take to keep improving?
2. We call maintaining our connectedness with other churches beyond our local church **interdependence**. Discuss and give examples of how the early church practiced interdependence among churches.
3. Even when the early church organized itself into "culturally conditioned forms" of Jewish and Gentile churches, they remained interdependent. How can your church maintain connectedness with other churches from other countries and cultures?
4. Discuss the seven biblical reasons why we maintain and practice interdependence. Which one stands out most to you? Which ones were new?
5. Discuss how in the Church of the Nazarene pastors are accountable to their churches and to superintendents, and superintendents are accountable to pastors and to each other. Do you feel this accountability is spiritually healthy? Why?

6. What are the dangers church leaders face when they are not in a family of churches that provides accountability?

7. Discuss how the Church of the Nazarene globally operates differently than Apple, Inc. Does this change the way you think about the church? How?

6

Cultivating Our Commitment to Multiply

"I tell you the truth, unless a kernel of wheat falls
to the ground and dies, it remains only a single seed.
But if it dies, it produces many seeds." (John 12:24)

Jesus was a master communicator. He knew the power of using short phrases to make a powerful point. He could take a complex issue and, using stories from everyday life, make statements and offer solutions to problems that are still being discussed 2,000 years later. One teaching of Jesus concerns the paradoxical relationship that exists between death and multiplication. "I tell you the truth," Jesus said, "unless a kernel of wheat falls to the ground and dies, it remains only a single seed. But if it dies, it produces many seeds" (John 12:24).

Death Precedes Multiplication

Jesus taught that the biblical key to multiplying the church is the sanctification of the church. Paul taught that God has promised to "sanctify us through and through" until our whole spirit, soul, and body are filled with the Holy Spirit and our agenda becomes the agenda of Jesus (1 Thessalonians 5:23-24). We believe this not only applies to individuals; it also applies to churches. Ironically, we cultivate our commitment to

> Jesus taught that the biblical key to multiplying the church is the sanctification of the church.

multiply when we are first willing to die (John 12:24). Death always precedes multiplication. This is not a new idea that has emerged in the 21st century—it is a principle Jesus taught over 2,000 years ago.

It is always the crucifixion of the church that fuels the multiplication of the church. This same thinking led the apostle Paul to write: "I have been crucified with Christ and I no longer live, but Christ lives in me" (Galatians 2:20). We have received and use the ecumenical creeds of the first five Christian centuries as expressions of our faith.[1] We must never forget, however, it was not the creeds that fueled the early expansion of the church—it was the blood of the martyrs. Those who were willing to follow Jesus to their own death revolutionized the world.[2] Whether for good or evil reasons, people who are willing to die fuel a movement.

> It was the blood of the martyrs that fueled the early expansion of the church...people who are willing to die fuel a movement.

One of the things that subtly changes within any movement that begins losing fuel, is the lack of conversation about crucifixion. It is not pleasant for us to die to our own plans and agendas. It is not easy for churches to die to their individual agendas, but when they do, promised miracles of multiplication will happen! We call this experience that happens within a church, "corporate sanctification."[3]

When a local church is sanctified, it sacrifices part or all of itself for multiplying the movement of God. Corporate sanctification happens every time a church parents a new church. It happens when a smaller church sees the potential of reaching outsiders and "gives itself away" to become a campus of a larger church. It happens when a local church goes through the pain of revitalizing and makes the agenda of Jesus to reach outsiders a priority. It happens every time a local congregation votes itself out of existence, takes its assets and invests them in a new church.[4] It happens when a local church sends money to fuel the global movement of God instead of spending money on itself. All of these are examples of a church practicing the "sanctification" Jesus teaches in John 12:24.

> The purpose of spiritual planning is not to get everyone in the church to agree with "our agenda" but for everyone to collectively seek the agenda of Jesus.

Only when we are willing to die to our own agendas can the agenda of Jesus multiply. The purpose of spiritual planning is **not** to get everyone in the church to agree with "our agenda" but for everyone to collectively seek the agenda of Jesus. He has promised to reveal himself to us as we humble ourselves and seek his grace (James 4:6).

We have always taught that repentance, brokenness, renewal, and an urgency to be different are not only for individuals, but something entire churches can enjoy. Where the movement of God through the people of God is breaking out at its highest levels is where local churches have learned to practice the teachings of Jesus regarding corporate sanctification.

The development of this attitude leads pastors and leaders to make church decisions driven not just by addition, but by missional multiplication.[5] For the last four thousand years of Judeo/Christian history, God's followers have been tempted to live by logic rather than obedience and faith. Thankfully, people who join multiplying movements believe in a God "who calls things that are not as though they already were" (Romans 4:17). Like Abraham, "they believe the Lord" (Genesis 15:6) and are "fully persuaded that God has the power to do what he has promised" (Romans 4:21).

Sanctification & Multiplication Principles

Once the Holy Spirit reminds us of what Jesus said (John 14:26), our eyes are opened and we begin to see biblical principles of both sanctification and multiplication. The following are ten principles for local churches and districts that are serious about healthy, multiplying churches. First, **only what we give away multiplies**. In the Gospels, we find Andrew standing beside a little boy with a little lunch. The crowd around them is five thousand men, plus women and children. It does not make logical sense that Jesus and his disciples could take this little boy's lunch and make something happen that no one would ever forget. "Here is a boy with five small barley loaves and two small fish, but how far will they go among so many?" (John 6:9)

> Only what we give away multiplies.

This is a powerful reminder that when our resources are given away and placed in the hands of Jesus, he can take and multiply them. Jesus taught: "Unless a kernel of wheat falls to the ground and dies, it remains only a single seed. But **if it dies**, it **produces** many seeds" (John 12:24). In the Kingdom of God, when we are willing to take what we have and give it away, Jesus can multiply it.

The enormous temptation churches face is to focus on addition—just **adding** to our own local ministry. There is certainly a time and place for that. But when we begin seeing "our Jerusalem, Judea and Samaria" (Acts 1:8) the way Jesus sees it, we realize the task is far too big for one ministry or one local church. As we grow the Kingdom where God has placed us, we need to remember what Jesus modeled for us—only what we give away multiplies.

The second principle is that **multiplication is the key to spiritually feeding everyone.** John 6:12 says, "they all had enough to eat."

> Multiplication is the key to spiritually feeding everyone.

As biblical Christians, we have a deep passion to spiritually feed the world. Jesus is the bread of life (John 6:35). Our challenge is, "How do we get this bread to the people who need it?" Nowhere is this principle more relevant than in the area of healthy, multiplying churches. When a God-called leader and a parent church empower a group of families to plant the Kingdom in an under-reached community or cultural group, something supernatural happens.

Giving people away is always a stretch—it is hard to invest good families in another location, campus or ministry. But when we as leaders submit our wills and agendas to Jesus and give God's people away, God can take the people we "plant" and multiply them—ten, twenty, thirty, fifty and sometimes even a hundred times what we sow (Matthew 13:23). In the gospel account, "everyone had enough to eat" because a little boy was willing to give away what he had to Jesus. Being willing to do that with the people and resources God gives us is the key to spiritually feeding everyone.

The third principle is that **Jesus expects fruitfulness**. Because people were hoping for a political kingdom (Luke 19:11), Jesus gave us the parable of the ten minas.[6] Here Jesus made clear that before his return, he expected his followers to be faithful and fruitful with the resources and talents they had been given (Luke 19:15-19). Today, some Christians struggle with Jesus' expectations of fruitfulness. The king (Jesus), seems really hard on the servant who buries the gifts and resources he has been given (Luke 19:20-24).

Why was Jesus so hard on this wicked servant? There are four reasons. 1) He didn't share his Master's agenda for the Kingdom. 2) He didn't trust his Master's agenda, and so he replaced it with his own. 3) His only concern was for himself. 4) He did nothing to use the gifts and resources he had been given.[7] As his servants, Jesus expects us to join his agenda. His agenda includes fruitfulness with what he gives us.

> Jesus expects his followers to be faithful and fruitful with the resources and talents they have been given.

The fourth principle is that **Jesus expects us to multiply what we have been given.** To explain his expectations, Jesus tells the parable of the talents (Matthew 25:14-30). In it he divides the talents among his servants according to their abilities. "To whom much is given, much is required" (Luke 12:48). No one receives more or less than he can handle (Matthew 25:15). Here Jesus is talking about any resources of time, talent or treasure that God has given us. He expects us to invest them wisely until he comes back, and he expects a return on that investment. Those who were loyal in using what they had been given were told, "well done, good and faithful servant" (Matthew 25:21,23).

The servant who only thought of himself, who played it safe, who only cared about protecting his own interests was called by Jesus "a wicked, lazy servant" (Matthew 25:26). He did not care about multiplying what he had been given. He forgot that the time, talent and treasure he had **did not belong to him**; it belonged to the Master. He was not an owner, only a steward and a manager of what **God owned.** To summarize, the agenda of Jesus includes multiplying what we have been given.

The fifth principle we find is that **God expects cooperation and interdependence to characterize his people**. We have already looked at examples of this in the New Testament—there are examples in the Old Testament as well. In Israel's history, there were some people filled with great faith (Numbers 13:25-32). God had given them the assurance of taking the Promised Land. Moses told them, "The

> God expects cooperation and interdependence among Christians.

Lord your God has given you this land to take possession of it. But all your able-bodied men, armed for battle, must cross over ahead of your brother Israelites...until the Lord gives rest to your brothers as he has to you, and they too have taken over the land that the Lord your God is giving them, across the Jordan. After that, each of you may go back to the possession I have given you" (Deuteronomy 3:18,20).

God wants us to learn lessons from Israel's history. "These things happened to them as examples and were written down for us" (1 Corinthians 10:11). Assisting our brothers in taking new territory is not a suggestion; it is God's command. The tribes on the east side of the Jordan had already received their inheritance. But God did not want them to settle down in comfort. There was more territory to conquer. God wanted every established leader to be involved in the "taking of new territory" process.

His promise was clear. "The Lord has given us territory to take possession of it" (Deuteronomy 3:18). God had promised territory multiplication! There was one way for that to happen. "All your able-bodied men, armed for battle" (the existing spiritual army), must be willing to cross over ahead of God's expanding work. God's plan is that churches not settle in the comfort and safety of their "own land," but maintain a spirit of interdependence. We need multiplying movement leaders who lead the way as parent churches, cooperating to multiply God's church. We all work together "until the Lord gives rest to our brothers" just as he has to us (Deuteronomy 3:20). God expects a spirit of cooperation and interdependence to reign among us as we lock arms to multiply his Kingdom on districts throughout the world.

The sixth principle is that **Jesus lived with a "next town" mentality.** After beginning his ministry, Jesus knew he needed to regularly experience spiritual renewal and receive instruction from his heavenly Father. After long days of healing and spending time with masses of people (Mark 1:33), Jesus needed direction. So "very early in the morning, while it was still dark, Jesus got up, left the house and went off to a solitary place, where he prayed" (Mark 1:35).

The disciples came looking for Jesus, and everyone else was looking for him as well. In those early morning hours, Jesus received clear instruction; his Father wanted him to have a "next town" mentality (Luke 4:43). He was not just to plant the Kingdom where he was, but to plant it in the **next town**, among the next people group. Jesus was never content with planting his Kingdom message in one location. As we study his ministry carefully, Jesus modeled an incredible multiplication mentality.

> Jesus was never content with planting his Kingdom message in one location.

When his body, the church, commits to help sponsor a new church in another community or under-reached people group, its members are following the mentality Jesus models here in the Gospels. "Let us go somewhere else...this is why I have come" (Mark 1:38). Jesus lived with a clear "next town" mentality.

The seventh principle is that **Jesus developed leaders, delegating authority and responsibility to them**. Jesus provided ongoing training as he lived with his disciples. He did not wait for them to finish classes before the practice of ministry began. From the beginning he spent time with them,[8] did ministry as they watched him serve, then followed up with a time of debriefing.

After a few months of ministry, Jesus called the Twelve to himself, delegated power and authority to them, and sent them out to preach (Luke 9:1-2). Just a short time later, Jesus appointed seventy-two other leaders and sent them out two-by-two to do ministry (Luke 10:1).

> ### Jesus planned his ministry so it could be easily multiplied by others.

When they returned and reported their activities, Jesus gave them spiritual encouragement (Luke 10:17-24), and celebrated in prayer these leaders that his Father was developing! The leadership development process Jesus followed, giving away authority and responsibility, is much like Paul training Timothy as his apprentice.

The leader development pattern Jesus practiced was simple, because he always operated with a multiplication mentality. He planned his ministry so it could be easily multiplied by others. The pattern he used was something like this:

Step 1: I do. You watch. We talk.

Step 2: I do. You help. We talk.

Step 3: You do. I help. We talk.

Step 4: You do. I watch. We talk.

Step 5: You do. Someone else watches. They talk.

Where healthy, multiplying churches happen, leaders are raising up their Timothys and developing them by giving away both authority and responsibility (2 Timothy 2:2).

The eighth principle is that **Jesus** is always the **primary disci-**

pler, not us. If the Timothy leaders God raises up among us become too dependent on our leadership, the church is weakened and the movement of God sputters. This is one of the reasons Jesus only stayed on earth for three years. He did not want the disciples to become dependent on him in the flesh. He wanted them to become dependent on the Spirit whom the Father promised would come. The Trinity was going to fill them and guide them. They were never going to be orphans and left to do ministry by themselves (John 14:18-26). He told them, "I will be with you to the end of the age" (Matthew 28:20).

> Jesus wanted his disciples to become dependent on the Spirit whom the Father promised would come, not on him in the flesh.

We are never alone, and the new leaders the Lord raises up are never alone. Jesus will lead them, guide them, and disciple them if they learn to listen to his voice for their lives and ministry (John 10:27). Jesus describes this fully when he explains the activity of the Holy Spirit to his disciples in John 14:1-17:26. After a while, our Timothys will not need us because we have taught them how to remain connected with Jesus as the head of the church. This requires us to remember that Jesus is always the primary discipler, not us.

The ninth principle is that **as they begin, new churches should cultivate their own commitment to multiply.** As we have participated in training hundreds of church planters, we have watched many of them on the receiving end of parent church sacrifice. Jesus taught, "It is more blessed to give than to receive" (Acts 20:35). This is why, early on, we encourage church planters to cultivate their own commitment to multiply. As church planting momentum builds within a district, new churches can help lead the way by parenting or sponsoring a new church. God is pleased whenever cooperation, interdependency, and loyalty to the parent church pastor and district are present in the planter.

There are many planters who have few resources as they begin: no building, little money and few members. Should we ask them to make this same commitment to multiply in some way following their launch? The answer is yes. We have learned healthy church multiplication is not a members or money issue. It is a heart issue. God's Kingdom needs visionary, interdependent planters who fuel the movement of God. Every district needs dozens of healthy, multiplying churches with leaders who cultivate their commitment to multiply, linking arms to reach people Jesus came to save (Luke 19:10).

The tenth principle is that leaders should help **nurture a spiritual climate that produces parent churches.** The church at Antioch had a clear multiplying mission. Church leaders knew not every person who needed Christ would join the Antioch church. They realized the measure of a great church was not its **seating capacity** but its **sending capacity.** They understood what Paul later wrote, "How can they believe in the one of whom they have not heard? And how can they hear without someone preaching to them? And how can they preach unless they are sent?" (Romans 10:14-15). It was in an atmosphere of worshiping the Lord and fasting that the Holy Spirit spoke about releasing two leaders as the first official church planters of the Christian faith (Acts 13:2).

> The measure of a great church is not its **seating** capacity but its **sending** capacity.

The spiritual climate at Antioch was what led this congregation to become the first parent church. Its members were sensitive, prepared, and ready to obey what the Holy Spirit told them to do. Today, they are the New Testament model for parent churches worldwide. They had agenda harmony and the spiritual climate was right. The church embraced the agenda of Jesus, and the result was a parent church sending service. "So after they had fasted and prayed, they placed their hands on Barnabas and Saul and sent them off" (Acts 13:3).

The Antioch church shows us how a parent church/church planting sending service can be conducted: with fasting, prayer, and the laying on of hands. The Antioch members gathered around Paul and Barnabas, laid hands on them, communicating their love, support and genuine care. As a parent church, we can never underestimate the value of a word or personal touch. Church planters need to feel loved and supported in the same kind of climate that was present at Antioch.

> Healthy churches focus on creating a spiritual climate that produces parent churches.

God wants hundreds of local churches to sponsor and parent new churches, just like the church at Antioch did. If the leaders focus on creating a climate that produces parent churches, they have the promise that God will open many new doors of faith (Acts 14:27).

Thinking Like A Missionary Fuels Multiplication

As we begin thinking like missionaries, we cannot ignore or simplify the complexity of the culture around us. Communities are becoming multi-cultural melting pots all over the globe, filled with hundreds of sub-cultures. Culture is never static; it is constantly changing. It is usually pluralistic and influenced by the other sub-cultures around it.

Leaders in healthy, multiplying churches learn to think like cross-cultural missionaries. They become familiar with the language, customs, and worldview of the people they are trying to reach. They "exegete" the culture just as much as they exegete the Scriptures they seek to share. This was the practice of Paul when he exegeted the religious thinking of the Athenians and began his presentation by referring to "the unknown God" (Acts 17:23).

Because most churches today are located in a post-Christian culture, effective pastors help their church leaders develop the ability to understand post-Christian ways of thinking. As church members begin thinking like missionaries, they care about learning how the world around them "thinks." They want to develop a contagious church culture designed to embrace outsiders who are not yet Christians. They want to create safe environments where people can ask honest questions as they begin their journey toward faith.

> Missionaries know God is already doing more underneath than they can see on the surface. God is drawing people to himself.

Missionaries are patient. Because they believe in the prevenient grace of God, they know God is already doing more underneath than they can see on the surface. God is drawing people to himself.[9] Missionaries tolerate the "mess" that comes with embracing outsiders. They don't expect people to think or behave like Christians until they become Christians.

A brief read of the New Testament reveals that the early church was a very messy movement. Read the book of 1 Corinthians. Paul planted the church at Corinth, and its cultural context shaped the way he led the church to maturity as he taught them to embrace "the most excellent way" (1 Corinthians 12:31).

In 1989, the United States and Canada was declared a mission field by the church. Each one of us is living in a mission field. Our districts are mission fields. Because of this, district leaders now encourage every church, every pastor, every lay person to begin thinking like a missionary. The church as we have known it is changing. The world around us is changing. We all see it, feel it, pray about it, and as church leaders, we come together and talk about it. We know the church must continue to change if we are to make a great impact in all the diverse communities and cultures within our districts.

> The church as we have known it is changing. The world around us is changing. We all see it, feel it and pray about it. We come together and talk about it.

The church is multiplying globally because many in our global church think like missionaries. Many global Nazarenes have a practical ecclesiology—they behave out of what they believe. They believe deeply in both spiritual crucifixion and the multiplication of the church.

Harnessing the Power of the Nazarene Network

Nazarenes have become very effective in multiplying churches because we have learned to harness the power of our global Nazarene network. There are unique features embedded in our Nazarene polity which help fuel our movement. We are deeply loyal in our love for the church. We follow Jesus' call to practice servant leadership. **There is no higher office in the church than that of an ordained elder.** We elect General Superintendents to lead the church globally. They are HIGHLY respected, but we have no popes or bishops among us. We simply have different roles and responsibilities. Everyone is on **one team** and each person is empowered to make a unique contribution.

Nazarenes have consciously developed a model of church that differs from the Protestant norm. In 1980, we adopted a policy of internationalization where churches and districts constitute a world-wide fellowship of believers with full acceptance of everyone within their cultural contexts. We embrace a single connectional framework and reject any mentality that evaluates people and nations in terms of "strong and weak, donor and recipient." In this way, our church is unique in its global view.

Millennials especially love the way we look at the world—we recognize the strengths and equality of churches and leaders from every country, regardless of economic capacity.[10] As participants in a global community of believers, we share the values of Christian, Holiness, Missional, and connectional. We have learned that the multiplication of the church happens faster if no person or group tries to control it. As the world changes and global communication increases, pastors and superintendents collaborate globally. We operate an open community of believers where every leader shares the agenda of Jesus to fuel a holiness, Great Commission movement.

> Millennials especially love the way we look at the world—we recognize the strengths and equality of churches and leaders from every country, regardless of economic capacity.

Our open, global community does not centralize intelligence or information. Instead, the intelligence and information are spread throughout our Nazarene network. Information and knowledge naturally filter in at the edges because the important learning we need to fuel the movement usually comes from local churches, where Christlike disciple-making happens.

As a church, we aim to capture, catalogue and communicate our learning globally, especially in the area of church development. As we observe the church multiplying throughout the world, it usually happens because God raises up a catalyzer to lead a church planting movement on one of our districts. The stories we hear of church and district multiplication fuel our hearts toward greater WEF (World Evangelism Fund) giving!

> Our global network is a gift of the Holy Spirit. This is our century. Now is our time.

We are moving into a different world, a new world. Here is the great news! As Nazarenes we are prepared to embrace the mission of Jesus in the 21st century like no other church. Our global network is a gift of the Holy Spirit. This is our century. Now is our time. The movement of God through the people of God needs you **today** to help cultivate a commitment to multiply where you serve.

Questions for Reflection—Chapter 6

1. Discuss this idea that Jesus taught: "death always precedes multiplication." How does this spiritual principle apply to what happened in the history of the early church?

2. What do you know about the first three centuries of the Christian faith? Have you ever heard of the term, "the blood of the martyrs?" Pause and take a few moments to pray for persecuted Christians around the world.

3. Every Christian in the world believes in individual "sanctification" because the Bible teaches it. However, many churches are yet to discover and practice the biblical principle of corporate sanctification. What are some examples of "corporate sanctification" the authors discuss? Does your church practice any of these? How might your church begin doing so?

4. The authors give ten principles of both sanctification and multiplication. Which ones impacted you the most? What did you learn? Were there any principles you had never heard of or did not know?

5. As you reflect on this chapter, how can your church not just add to your own ministry but begin to give away so you can multiply?

6. Does this chapter help you understand how spiritual movements grow from a small beginning to tens of thousands? Discuss how the Church of the Nazarene has practiced these principles and grown from a handful of churches to 30,000+ churches in 160+ countries. How does this make you feel about the church? Who can you share these principles with, so the movement continues to spread?

7. Discuss the following statement: "**There is no higher office in the church than that of an ordained elder**. We have no popes or bishops among us. We simply have different roles and responsibilities." How can we do a better job of making every person in the church feel like they are a vital part of the team, working together for the good of the church?

8. Understanding these multiplication principles and the global network of the church, do you agree with the authors that the Church of the Nazarene is positioned like no other church to make an impact in the 21st century? Why?

7

Building A Contagious Church Culture

"Then the Lord replied: 'Write down the vision and make it plain on tablets so that a messenger may run with it. For the vision awaits an appointed time; it speaks of the end and will not prove false. Though it linger, wait for it; it will certainly come and will not delay…but the righteous will live by faith.'" (Habakkuk 2:2-4)

Effective leaders know that while we clarify mission, develop vision and build strategy, **changing the culture** of a church is the most important objective we face in shaping a great future. It is our culture that determines the receptivity of leaders to new ideas. It is our culture that unleashes creativity, builds enthusiasm, fosters encouragement and creates a sense of ownership as we work together. Ultimately, it is the culture of a church that shapes individual morale, teamwork, effectiveness, and directly impacts our long-term health and capacity to multiply.

> The way people are treated, the way people treat their peers within the church, the way people respond to church leaders and church operations…all of this is the "air" of a church that people breathe.

What do we mean by church culture? It is not a simple thing to define. It includes things we can see, like the way people dress and behave, the look of the office and the pictures and messages we put on the walls. It includes our values, both stated and unstated, our beliefs and assumptions, not just doctrinal beliefs but operational beliefs. How is spiritual health celebrated? How are problems addressed? How do we demonstrate trust and respect for each other?

Culture is deeper than vision or strategy and harder to shape and change because culture is about relationships and people. The way people are treated, the way people treat their peers within the church, the way people respond to church leaders and church operations...all of this is the "air" of a church that people breathe. If we make sure that air is healthy and invigorating, our church will thrive. If that "air" gets stagnant or discouraging, the agenda harmony will subside, creativity will lag, seeds of apathy will germinate, and the culture of the church will lack spiritual momentum.[1] In other words, the "air" quality we breathe together is really important!

Desire, Resources and Climate

After conversations with numerous pastors and superintendents, there are three things that seem to be foundational in building a contagious church culture. We refer to them as the "three circles."[2]

> Desire is the **"want to,"** resources are the **"how to,"** and climate is the **"get to"** in building a contagious church culture.

Part of our discovery is that desire, resources, and climate are all essential in developing a healthy, multiplying church.

Building a contagious church culture takes not one or two but all three circles of desire, resources, and climate, integrated together. Desire is the **"want to,"** resources are the **"how to,"** and climate is the **"get to."** The integration of all three circles is essential for a contagious church culture to be built.

As illustrated below, fruitlessness, futility, and frustration are all the result when only two of the three circles are present. When desire and resources are present but there is no development of climate, the result is **fruitlessness.** When resources and a beginning climate are present but there is no desire in the heart of key leaders, the result is **frustration** for people who want to see the Kingdom move forward. When desire and a beginning climate are present but there are no resources, the result is a feeling of **futility**. The heart of building a contagious church culture is found in the center, when all three—desire, resources, and climate come together. The diagram below illustrates this.

The good things that happen in a local church begin with **desire.** Leaders who develop desire begin to seek the **knowledge** they need. They develop the **vision** that motivates them and others to facilitate change. They are willing to be vulnerable and open with their team, defining the current reality and investing the time needed to build **trust**. The circle of desire includes knowledge, vision, and trust.

Desire begins with **knowledge**. God says, "my people are destroyed for lack of knowledge" (Hosea 4:6). Many leaders want to enjoy the benefits of a healthy, multiplying church, but they do not understand how to get there from the current reality they face. Their future is being "destroyed" simply because of what they do not know. It may be knowledge about how to change the climate, how to build agenda harmony, how to do a church assessment, how to take necessary steps to revitalize the church, how to develop deeper relationships of trust or how to develop systems for evangelism and leader development.

> Here is the good news. Everything you as a leader need to be effective, serving where God has placed you, **can be learned!**

Here is the good news. Everything you as a leader need to be effective, serving where God has placed you, **can be learned!** The humility that allows us to learn from leaders who are different from us is essential. The desire for life-long learning is the foundation of receiving the knowledge we need. Leaders of healthy, multiplying churches have teachable spirits. They are hungry to be taught, corrected and trained. "All Scripture is God-breathed and is **useful for** teaching, rebuking, **correcting** and **training** in righteousness" (2 Timothy 3:16).

Leaders who desire to build a contagious church culture have spiritually matured and have no ego to protect. The knowledge they seek can be learned from anyone and everyone. They deeply **desire** to be taught, trained, and corrected. Do you remember being corrected when you were a child? Did you love it? You probably did not. Paul writes, "When I was a child…I thought like a child, I reasoned like a child. When I became a man, I put the ways of childhood behind me" (1 Corinthians 13:11).

Maturity in leadership requires us to leave the "ways of child-hood." As leaders, we must embrace a life-long commitment to learning, correction, and training. The Scriptures explain that if we ignore correction, we will lead others astray (Proverbs 10:17); if we hate correction, we are senseless (Proverbs 12:1), and if we heed correction, we will be honored (Proverbs 13:18). Mockers resent correction and will not consult those who are wise (Proverbs 15:12). Whoever heeds correction gains understanding (Proverbs 15:32).

> Leaders who want to build a contagious church culture have a deep desire to be taught, trained and corrected.

It is God's Word within us that cultivates this desire to grow and learn, rather than maintain the status quo. Many leaders serving in churches that need change must begin to replace their current habits with new thinking and desire that lead them to be different. "If you had responded to my rebuke, I (wisdom) would have poured out my heart to you and made my thoughts known to you" (Proverbs 1:23). "Fools are headstrong and do what they like; wise people take advice" (Proverbs 12:15, Msg).

"If you correct those who care about life…they'll love you for it!" (Proverbs 9:8, Msg). "Give instruction to the wise, and they will become wiser still; teach the righteous and they will gain in learning" (Proverbs 9:9, NRSV). "The wise in heart accept commands" (Proverbs 10:8).

At this point, we ask that you be totally honest before God (Hebrews 4:13). As a leader, how much desire do you have to seek the knowledge you need for participating in a healthy, multiplying church?

> How deep is your desire to be corrected and changed by Jesus? How willing are you to learn, grow and receive the knowledge you do not now have?

How deep is your desire to be corrected and changed by Jesus? How willing are you to learn, grow and receive the knowledge you do not now have?

There is a direct relationship between healthy, multiplying churches and a deep desire by their leaders to be teachable. Leaders who become highly effective develop the private habits they need to change, learn and grow. **They seek knowledge**—they have a deep desire to be corrected and trained **in any way** that makes them wiser and more effective. "The Word is in their heart like a burning fire…they cannot hold it in" (Jeremiah 20:9) and they cannot stay the same. Because of the Word in them, status quo is not acceptable.

If your heart is beating fast right now, because the Spirit inside you testifies with your spirit that this is true (1 John 5:6-9) and you are in agreement, believe today that Jesus has the power to make your future different than your past! You can become a renewed, vital part of fueling the movement of God through the people of God where you serve.

> Believe today that Jesus has the power to make your future different than your past!

The Holy Spirit can teach you and remind you of everything Jesus wants you to learn (John 14:26). Cultivate humility because the Spirit may surprise you regarding the source of your needed knowledge. As the Holy Spirit births desire within us, we gain understanding through other people who have been on the journey before us. We never stop networking with other leaders who are willing to help us learn. "When the student is ready, the teacher will appear."[3] The circle of desire always begins with a thirst for knowledge. Our development of knowledge leads us to pray and seek God's vision.

> As the Holy Spirit births desire within us, we gain understanding through other people who have been on the journey before us. We never stop networking with other leaders who are willing to help us learn.

Desire builds with **vision.** The development of vision for a church follows our exposure to knowledge. If God had his full way and the church experienced incredible health, what would look different? What would be different? How would people think and act? If God moved in a great way and did "immeasurably more than we could ask or imagine" (Ephesians 3:20), how would we know it happened? If God supernaturally worked within our church and the culture was transformed, what would be different?

The vision for a different future always begins in the heart of a leader. That is just the beginning…It cannot stay there. It must become a "shared vision" through building agenda harmony. One of the greatest gifts a leader can give those who follow is a mental picture and vision description of the future that is different from the present.

This kind of vision does not come all at once. It takes time to develop, much like needing binoculars to see something five hundred yards away. We think we see it and we begin to walk toward it. It is always fuzzy at first, but it becomes clearer and clearer as time goes on.

The vision continues to be perfected as it is shared with the leadership team. God reminds us, "Write it down and make it plain…if it lingers, wait for it…it will certainly come" (Habakkuk 2:2-3).

Once **knowledge** is present and **vision** becomes clearer, the building of **trust** on the team is also essential. In the Old Testament, David did this by assigning **positions of trust** to his "gatekeepers" (1 Chronicles 9:22). In his book, *The Five Dysfunctions of a Team*, Patrick Lencioni observes that trust is one of the most powerful traits in shaping a positive culture, and trust thrives on honesty. He writes, "When there is an absence of trust, it stems from a leader's unwillingness to be vulnerable with the group. Leaders who are not genuinely open with one another about their mistakes and weaknesses make it impossible to build a foundation of trust."[4]

We build trust by being honest with one another. We tell positive stories. We celebrate heroes. We try to listen and learn all the time. We ask for input from people as we let the team shape the future. We encourage creativity and pray for enthusiasm. The integrity of leaders, their competence and the care they show for every person on the team—these are the things that build trust.

> We build trust by being honest with one another. We tell positive stories. We celebrate heroes. We try to listen and learn all the time.

The first circle of **desire** is our "want to." It includes knowledge, vision and trust. The second circle relates to our **resources.** This circle includes **people, systems & training,** and **stewardship.** Some church leaders mistakenly think that the most important resource we have relates to our finances, but this is not the case. The most important part of the church is always our **people**. They are never a commodity to be expended or replaced.

People know whether they are being used or respected and valued. We must care about people and "lay down our lives for them as a good shepherd" (John 10:11). People do not care how much we know until they know how much we care. Healthy churches build agenda harmony with a team of people. They know they are called by God and believe in what he is leading them to do. The foundation of every healthy church begins with **people**.

Once we have identified people to serve on the leadership team, we must build **systems** and provide **training** for them. We will address systems for church development in Book 2 of the **MULTIPLYNAZ** series. Excellent training tools now abound for our 480+ districts to use as we train and resource our pastors and lay leaders.

As superintendents work with pastors and church boards, they are always training, both formally and informally. They help leaders create church development plans. They provide mentoring and build systems of accountability for the implementation of those plans. Mentoring to encourage the church to move forward can be done by a variety of mentors. As pastors and lay leaders pray, seek the mind of Christ, and do spiritual planning, agenda harmony begins to build among them.

With people, systems and training in place, the circle of resources also requires stewardship. As we discussed in chapter 3, contagious churches are generous churches and high-expectation churches. Stewardship includes our time, talents, and treasure (finances). Jesus talked often about money, and because the church's mission is so important, healthy churches teach stewardship and raise money for ministry. Jesus used people with pure hearts and willing hands, but he also needed people to travel with him "and help support his disciples out of their own means" (Luke 8:3).

The agenda of Jesus and his mission required raising financial resources. Jesus boldly talked about the way people should manage the money God entrusted to them. He taught that we are stewards of every-thing we have, not owners.

Local churches with desire, vision, and trust experience the mi-raculous as they obey what the Scriptures teach regarding stewardship and generosity in giving. Where there is agenda harmony, shared vi-sion, and hope for the future, there are resources and power that emerge in the present. The second circle of **resources** is our "how to." It in-cludes people, systems and training, and stewardship.

The third circle involves the **climate** of a church. Some people use "climate" and "culture" interchangeably; we do not. We believe cli-mate is one of the factors that contributes to a change of culture. If we fuel a change of climate, over time the culture of a church will change. We have discovered there are three components that fuel a change of climate: believing prayer, spiritual planning, and agenda harmony.

Everything Begins with Believing Prayer

Believing prayer is where everything begins in a church. Many Christians pray, but their prayer life does not operate at a faith lev-el where they practice "believing prayer." They would benefit greatly from following the example of a father who came to Jesus. His son struggled with an impure spirit nearly all his life.

He pleaded with Jesus, "If you can do anything, take pity on us and help us." 'If you can?' said Jesus. "**Everything is possible for one who believes**." Immediately the boy's father exclaimed, "I do believe; help me overcome my unbelief!" (Mark 9:22-24) Our faith grows when we practice believing prayer. "Faith comes by hearing, and hearing by the word of God" (Romans 10:17, NKJV). Building faith is what Jesus planted in the hearts of his disciples, and it is also what a leader plants in the heart of a healthy, multiplying church.

After spending time with Jesus, the early disciples quickly recognized their need. They asked Jesus for help in the "faith area" of disciple-making. They said, "Lord, increase our faith!" (Luke 17:5) As followers of Jesus, we recognize our same need. This is our prayer as Nazarenes hungry for Jesus to increase our faith today! We believe he is the head of the church. He is alive and well, directing his Bride to depend on him and practice "believing prayer" all over the world.

> After spending time with Jesus, the early disciples quickly recognized their need. They asked Jesus for help... "Lord, increase our faith!"

A critical objective of our church has always been "the simplicity and spiritual power manifest in the New Testament Church."[5] What did the early church do? They practiced believing prayer. They understood that spending time with Jesus was the key. As we spend time with Jesus in prayer, his will, his Spirit, his values, his agenda and his heart begin to seep into our hearts. We begin to realize that what he said about the spiritual realm really is true— "with God all things are possible" (Matthew 19:26). We are never alone! (Matthew 28:20) He is with us! (Matthew 18:20)

What was the "spirit" that fueled the early church? Where did they get their spiritual power? Luke explains, "When they saw the courage of Peter and John and realized that they were unschooled, ordinary men, they were astonished and they took note that these men had been with Jesus" (Acts 4:13). Spending time with Jesus taught them they needed more faith! (Luke 17:5) They needed more time listening to and talking with the Heavenly Father (Luke 11:1). As they watched Jesus operate, they saw the power that flowed into his life from God as he practiced believing prayer.

Jesus is our example. Our mission is to make Christlike disciples who follow him. We pursue his heart, seek to be filled with his Spirit, read his Word, search for his agenda and come together with other like-minded believers. His agenda begins to create agenda harmony among us as we pray. We long for no other agenda except his. There is nothing in the world like the Spirit of Jesus dwelling in a church that practices believing prayer!

> As we spend time with Jesus in prayer, his will, his Spirit, his values, his agenda and his heart begin to seep into our hearts.

This kind of prayer includes learning to pray until we receive the assurance that God will answer us and show us what we now do not know (Jeremiah 33:3). It includes praying specifically (Matthew 6:11, Mark 10:51). It includes learning that we do not receive because we do not ask (Matthew 7:7). Sometimes we do not ask with the right motives (James 4:2-3). It includes learning to be persistent in our praying. Jesus taught that there is a direct relationship between faith and persistence. When he returns, he wants to find faith alive and well among us (Luke 18:1-8).

When we have sanctified hearts and only want Jesus' agenda, not ours, "This is the confidence we have in approaching God: that if we ask anything according to his will, he hears us. And if we know that he hears us—whatever we ask—**we know that we have what we asked of him**" (1 John 5:14-15).

Believing prayer changes the climate of a church. Believing prayer brings the presence of God into the midst of his people. "Divine power always follows divine presence. The Bible, from Genesis to Revelation, is filled with stories of how prayer brings God's power. Jesus promised his disciples that power would be the first fruit of our waiting and praying for the Holy Spirit"[6] (Acts 1:4,8). The practice of believing prayer looks different in different churches. In larger churches prayer may happen among leaders and also throughout the church in small groups. In smaller churches it can be a corporate prayer gathering which includes everyone. Some larger churches also follow this approach.

Whatever the process used, gaining agenda harmony with Jesus through believing prayer lies at the heart of all healthy churches. This is not our church; it belongs to Jesus. He is the head of it. His agenda must run it. We seek his agenda and what he wants through prayer. Later in the **MULTIPLYNAZ** series, we will talk about how prayer is the engine room of the church and how believing prayer creates the climate for church revitalizing and renewal. Churches that build spiritual momentum understand that everything begins with believing prayer.

In Book 2 of the **MULTIPLYNAZ** series, we will also talk about spiritual planning and how healthy, multiplying churches realize they do not know everything they need to know. This drives them to seek the knowledge they do not have from other leaders and churches. In the church development process, they move from dependence, through independence to interdependence. When believing prayer, spiritual planning and church development come together, it produces agenda harmony with amazing results.

Under the leadership of the Holy Spirit, when a church cultivates the "soil" by developing the right disciple-making habits, and when people begin experiencing divine moments with God, that church becomes unstoppable (Acts 2:42-47)! They move ahead with joy and optimism because everyone in the church senses they have a great future together. Jesus is alive and they know it (Acts 4:20). When these three circles of **desire, resources**, and **climate** all align in a local church, they fuel the beginning of a contagious culture.

Linking Passion with Planning

Wherever there is a contagious culture, a group of people live with passion. It has nothing to do with personality, emotion or temperament. Whether outgoing or quiet and behind-the-scenes, they deeply desire to know where Jesus is leading them. Like Paul, "they labor, struggling with all **God's energy,** which so powerfully works in them" (Colossians 1:29). They regularly remind themselves "to **fan into flame** the gift of God, which is within them" (2 Timothy 1:6). They know "the fire must be **kept burning** on the altar continuously; it must not go out" (Leviticus 6:13).

> When these three circles of desire, resources and climate all align in a local church, they fuel the beginning of a contagious culture.

In a healthy, multiplying church, leaders **link their passion with planning.** There can and should be no doubt in your mind that, with God's power, he can achieve through you the spiritual desires he is placing in your heart. God would not have given you these specific, Christ-centered desires for a healthy, multiplying church unless he knew you were capable of achieving them.

Every Christian leader has the potential of being personally led by the Holy Spirit. The Holy Spirit distributes spiritual gifts and abilities "just as he determines" (1 Corinthians 12:11). Paul teaches that our abilities and the Spirit's leadings modify our desires. "God is at work **in you,** to **will** and to **do**, according to his good purpose" (Philippians 2:13). Centered in God's will, the desire he has put in you for a healthy, multiplying church can and should become a reality! To aid you in the development of God's passion within you, the following are some practical steps you can take to bring God's vision into existence.

Begin this process with prayer and waiting on God. Do not just talk to God about it; listen for God's voice. Ask him to build your faith.

> Centered in God's will, the desire he has put in you for a healthy, multiplying church can and should become a reality!

Record any ideas or impressions God gives you as you seek his wisdom. In private, be definite about what you believe God wants you and your leadership team to do. Be wise about **when** and **what** you share. Joseph had the right dream, but he had horrible timing in sharing it (Genesis 37:5-11).

Ask yourself the question, "If we go after the vision God is beginning to place within us, what part does God expect **us** to play in achieving it? What part must **God** do?" This becomes your believing prayer list as you seek the divine moments you need from God. There is also a part **we play** in this process. Never forget, there is someone, somewhere who will help you fulfill God's vision and get your prayers answered. Everything can change in one day. Pray that you will be at the right place, at the right time, to meet the right person, so that together you can fulfill God's plan.

> There is someone, somewhere who will help you fulfill God's vision and get your prayers answered.

A key part of this process is also your commitment to create a detailed plan for achieving the vision God is giving you. With as much detail as you can, write everything down. Dr. J.B. Chapman wrote years ago, "Thoughts disentangle themselves when they pass through the lips and the fingertips." As you write the details of the plan, remember it will never be a static plan. It will always continue to adjust and change. You cannot wait until the plan is perfect to begin. There is no perfect plan. Do not procrastinate or wait for God to begin his part. He is waiting to see if you are serious about your part!

> Everything can change in one day. Pray that you will be at the right place, at the right time, to meet the right person, so that together you can fulfill God's plan.

After you begin, regularly review the plan God has given you. Keep perfecting it. Seek to be led by the Lord in his will. As his Spirit confirms his plans to you, see in your mind's eye, feel in your heart and believe with your will that your God-given desires have already begun to be fulfilled. God himself is big enough to make it happen! "The one who calls you is faithful, and he will do it" (1 Thessalonians 5:24).

Through the power of a God-given vision and the spiritual desire that God grants to those who long for it, God can and does give to people who seek it, that "**something within**" that recognizes no such word as impossible and spiritual power that accepts no such reality as failure.

> "Thoughts disentangle themselves when they pass through the lips and the fingertips."

Think Long-Term

It is an undeniable fact that the decisions made by leaders today greatly affect the church tomorrow. In the Scriptures, this is clearly seen in the life of Hezekiah. He was a leader who was only concerned about himself in the present. He was selfish, shortsighted and proud.

After he was healed of his sickness, representatives were sent by the rulers of Babylon to see his kingdom and ask how God had healed him. In reality, God was testing Hezekiah to see what was really in his heart and Hezekiah failed the test (2 Chronicles 32:31).

When the prophet Isaiah came to him and confronted him about his failure to think long-term, Hezekiah's only response was that he was happy he would be taken care of "in peace and security" during his lifetime (2 Kings 20:19). The lesson of Hezekiah applies to the church today. Lay leaders and pastors too often make decisions for the present, and the churches they serve reap the consequences, sometimes twenty or thirty years later.

For example, a highly influential lay leader may fight proposed changes that will reach outsiders…and win the battle. The church begins to decline because of this decision. Peace and security win over risk and opportunity. It can also be pastors who decide they are not interested in helping start new churches. The focus on planting new churches and new ministries erodes. Years later these decisions have a profound impact on the development of the healthy, multiplying movement that God desires.

> God does give to people who seek it that **"something within"** that recognizes no such word as impossible and spiritual power that accepts no such reality as failure.

Starting new churches is difficult work. Restarting a church can be messy. Revitalizing a church is a process filled with potential conflict and high degrees of criticism. Parenting a new church can require the sacrifice of members and money. As a church leader, it is easier to want "peace and security in my lifetime." It is more convenient to "let the leader who follows me handle the hassle." However, making a short-sighted decision today is choosing the decline of the church tomorrow.

> As a result of the decisions church leaders make today, the churches they serve reap the consequences of those decisions long after they are gone.

Our calling as church leaders is to make decisions today based on what is best for the church tomorrow, not what is best or easy for us. Dr. Bill Sullivan wrote, "The best time to plant a new tree was 20 years ago. The next best time is today."

Today is our day. In our church, we are not guided by a desire for peace and security; give us risk and opportunity! Leaders who are effective always think long-term. They know they are not bound to accept the current culture of the church as normal or a status quo church culture as inevitable. Filled with God's love, they build desire, gather needed resources, begin to change the climate, and over time, watch God build a contagious, new church culture.

The foundations that fuel a movement include leading with love, a focus on outsiders, clear beliefs about the church, practicing interdependence, cultivating our commitment to multiply and building a contagious church culture. Thank you for taking the time to not only read this book, but to reflect on the questions and talk with other church leaders about putting these

> We are not guided by a desire for peace and security; give us risk and opportunity!

ideas into practice. The Bible teaches we are not to be hearers only, but doers (James 1:22).

In Book 2 of the **MULTIPLYNAZ** series, we will discuss how God creates healthy, multiplying churches. We will discuss God's role in creating healthy churches, our Nazarene essentials, leaving no church behind, practicing spiritual planning, revitalizing and restarting, how healthy churches never stop learning, how healthy churches can grow large and more. We hope you will join us!

Questions for Reflection—Chapter 7

1. Is this the first time you have read about or discussed the "culture" of your church? What are the things we do or ways we behave that affect our culture?
2. Discuss the "three circles" of desire, resources, and climate. Why do the authors contend it is the integration of all three that produce a contagious culture? What happens when only two of the three are present?
3. The authors contend that the **desire** to develop God's church is fueled by three things: knowledge, vision, and trust. Do you agree with this? Why or why not?
4. The authors state that people who gain knowledge have a deep desire for life-long learning. They have teachable spirits and are hungry to be taught, corrected, and trained. What do you think are the factors that make some people hungry to learn and others to just want the status quo?

5. Discuss these questions using the following scale: on a scale of 1 to 10, (1 being very low desire and 10 incredibly high desire), how much desire do you have to participate in a healthy, multiplying church? How great is your desire to be corrected and changed by Jesus? How much desire do you have to learn, to grow and to receive the knowledge you do not now have? Share your thoughts with someone else and ask them to pray for you and with you.

6. The development of vision for a church follows our exposure to knowledge. If God had his full way and your church experienced incredible health, what would look different? What would be different? How would people think and act?

7. If God moved in a great way and did "immeasurably more than we could ask or imagine" (Ephesians 3:20), how would we know it happened? If God supernaturally worked within your church and the culture was transformed, what would look different? What would be different?

8. Read the believing prayer section on pages 128-131. What are your thoughts? What did you read about that was new? What stood out to you?

9. How would you describe your current "faith level?" Like the disciples, do you need Jesus to increase your faith? What needs to change so that you begin to believe and practice that "with God, all things are possible?"

10. Have you ever been part of a church where you experienced the Holy Spirit building agenda harmony through believing prayer? If so, what was it like? Share your thoughts with your group.

11. Have you ever been part of a church where desire, resources and climate all came together to create a contagious church culture? If so, describe the church to the other people in your group.

12. Read through the section entitled, "Linking Passion with Planning." What stood out to you? What was new to you? What did you learn about the importance of writing out a plan?

13. Why should leaders always think and act long-term?

14. Reflect on the next steps Jesus wants you to take. Now that you have a beginning understanding of the issues involved in building a contagious church culture, what is Jesus saying to you? What practical steps can you take to make the church where you serve a place that becomes "contagious"? Pray about this. Our prayers are with you as well. We are thankful for your love for the church.

Receiving Suggestions and Corrections

In the Preface, we shared that this book series is **not** complete. We want the series to have feedback and be shaped by MANY different participants. If we could, we would have EVERY pastor and lay leader participate in its writing. The church does not belong to a few; it belongs to everyone. Everyone should write the story and everyone is— all over the world. We wish we could share everything we are learning and publish every miracle that is happening around the world in our 30,000+ congregations.

Thank you so much for your involvement in the **MULTIPLYNAZ** writing project and for your willingness to critique and provide feedback. The standard we seek in everything we do is the same standard we find in the ministry of Jesus: "People were overwhelmed with amazement. 'He has done everything well,' they said" (Mark 7:37).

On the www.multiplynaz.org website under the **About** section, you will find a page called **Feedback**. There you can submit your suggestions or additions to any ideas found in the **MULTIPLYNAZ** series. We ask for your contact information, along with the particular book in the series, change needed/additional thought, and your feedback. You may also use this form to offer an endorsement.

This book has been reviewed by dozens of church leaders, many of whom have made suggestions and corrections for improvement. We have a never-ending commitment to keep on learning and refining as we move our collective writing forward with greater precision. We will read every word of every paragraph you send us. Again, THANKS for your participation.

A Global Resourcing Vision

Most people have heard of Wikipedia. Wikipedia is a multi-lingual online encyclopedia, based on open collaboration through a wiki-based content editing system. It is the largest and most popular general reference work on the worldwide web. It is also one of the most popular websites ranked by Alexa. It features exclusively free content, no commercial ads and is supported by a nonprofit organization funded primarily through donations.

In a perfect church world, we would have something multi-lingual and online like Wikipedia, but designed specifically for the development of healthy, multiplying Nazarene churches throughout the world. Districts and local churches would have a platform to resource one another around the vision for developing healthy, multiplying churches. We would establish a "common language" so that nothing we try to do would be impossible (Genesis 11:6). We would endeavor to follow the motto of the U.S. Army Corp of Engineers: "the difficult we do immediately, the impossible takes a little longer." This series of **MULTIPLYNAZ** books and websites is a humble first step.

Our movement of God through the people of God currently worships in 212 languages and we produce video and printed materials in 95 of these languages. Hundreds of books are produced in multiple languages for worship, evangelism training, discipleship training, leadership development, theology, etc. Helping to fuel everything we do is a clear, simple foundation put forth by our General Superintendents to "make Christlike disciples in the nations." **MULTIPLYNAZ** is just one of many church resources our movement has for creating healthy, multiplying Nazarene churches and districts. If something we have written helps fuel the Nazarene movement and resources healthy, multiplying Nazarene churches and districts, our purpose will have been achieved.

Again, we ALWAYS welcome your suggestions, feedback, corrections and improvements to the **MULTIPLYNAZ** book series and websites. Please send these via our website at www.multiplynaz.org. It is a privilege to be a partner in ministry with you. Our desire is to serve you with excellence in all we do. If there is any way we can do that better, please let us know. We have wonderful days ahead!

Subject Index

Scripture Index

Notes & Credits

Preface

[1] We believe the Holy Spirit alone is the one who unifies and calls the Church together through the Word (*Nazarene Manual,* par 11).

[2] Cultivating a spirit of interdependence lies at the heart of every one of our 480+ Nazarene districts throughout the world (*Nazarene Manual,* par 200). We want to capture, catalogue, and communicate best practices to improve the health of districts by increasing our understanding and practice of interdependence.

[3] This projection comes from a United Nations study. Countries use different terms to describe urban areas, cities, etc. As of this writing, the international Demographic report details there are now 1,050 identified urban areas worldwide with 500,000 or more population. These are the future mission fields for the movement of God through the people of God.

[4] This fulfills Nazarene Manual par 122 and 129.4, which state that a planning session should be conducted every year and the written results should be shared with the district. We suggest every church create a Church Development Plan and annually update the plan to celebrate progress.

How to Use This Book

[1] A big thank-you goes to Dr. Mark Berry for suggesting the inclusion of questions for reflection at the end of each chapter.

Introduction

[1] Jesus is called a Nazarene twelve times in the Scriptures. We find these in Mark 10:47, 14:67, 16:6; Luke 24:19; John 18:5, 18:7, 19:19; Acts 2:22, 3:6, 4:10, 6:14, 22:8. In several instances the translation says "Jesus of Nazareth" instead of Jesus the Nazarene but in all instances Jesus is referenced to be a Nazarene.

[2] Nazarene Board of General Superintendents (Lenexa, KS: Global Ministry Center, 2015). Nazarene Essentials is a summary of Nazarene teaching, history, theology, mission, funding and connections. See www.nazarene.org/essentials for a more complete summary of our history.

[3] From a sermon by David Busic, delivered at the NCM Global Compassion Conference at Olivet Nazarene University, July 14, 2016.

Chapter 1

[1] Every minister of the gospel who serves in the Church of the Nazarene is to live filled with the Holy Spirit, have a deep love for unbelievers and those currently outside the church. We believe those who have not received and trusted in Christ are perishing (John 1:12, 3:16) (Manual par 502.2).

[2] The Church of the Nazarene "is unapologetically connectional. By this we mean we are an interdependent body of local churches organized into districts in order to carry out our mutual mission of 'making Christlike disciples in the nations.' Our commitment is to be accountable to one another for the sake of the mission." This statement is located in "A Connected Church 1.1." and can be found on the web at www. nazarene.org/essentials.

[3] A list of the 65 participants who have, to date, added their thoughts to this writing project can be found on pages 3-9. The prayer of each one is that God will build agenda harmony within his church and the 21st century will be the greatest century of healthy, multiplying churches and districts that the church has ever known.

Chapter 2

[1] This statement is true, not only in the context of the persecution of the church, but also in how Christians represent the church. In today's political climate, we have seen social media strewn with posts in the name of Jesus, which are harmful to the church of Jesus Christ—and thus painful to Christ himself.

[2] Ecclesiology is a theological term for "the study of" (ology) the "church" (ecclesia).

[3] Spiritual insights in this section are adapted from a teaching by Pastor Rick Warren, Saddleback Valley Community Church, Lake Forest, CA.

Chapter 3

[1] Prevenient Grace is our VII Article of Faith: "We believe that the grace of God through Jesus Christ is freely bestowed upon all people, enabling all who will to turn from sin…" (Manual, Church of the Nazarene, par 7).

[2] W.T. Purkiser, Richard S. Taylor and Willard H. Taylor, *God, Man and Salvation—A Biblical Theology* (Kansas City, MO: Beacon Hill Press, 1977) p. 411.

[3] We encourage every Christian to study the 158 references in Scripture to God's favor and how he bestows it. We believe God grants people favor with him and with others. God's favor is foundational to all his work in the world.

[4] *God, Man and Salvation—A Biblical Theology*, p 411.

[5] Obstacles to Evangelism in the Local Church—Rainer on Leadership #108, March 20, 2015 podcast. Visit www.thomrainer.com for more information.

[6] *God, Man and Salvation—A Biblical Theology*, p. 136.

[7] The Nazarene Manual allows churches to use alternative board and committee structures to organize for ministry and missional action, provided such alternatives are approved in writing by the District Superintendent and the District Advisory Board (Manual par 113.12).

[8] Thanks goes to Jon Hauser, founder of Prairie Heights Community Church in Fargo, North Dakota, for providing insights in chapter three

related to churches keeping their focus on outsiders.

[9] Discipleship as a journey of grace is the focus of the global SDMI (Sunday School and Discipleship Ministries International) led by Scott Rainey. A major contribution to this section of the book came from him.

Chapter 4

[1] *Nazarene Manual*, 2017 – 2021, par 11, p 33.

[2] This statement is located in "Our Nazarene Characteristics 1.1."and can be found on the web at www.nazarene.org/essentials.

[3] In addition to our evangelism focus every day of the week, (Acts 2:47), there is value in emphasizing the sacredness of the Lord's Day. In Western culture, Sunday has increasingly lost its connection to Christian tradition. The problem is not "tradition" for its own sake, but the evangelistic embodiment of a people who treat the Lord's Day so distinctly that it opens positive, spiritual conversations with our neighbors (insight provided by Dr. Jeren Rowell).

[4] Visit www.multiplynaz.org under the models section for a list of different church models the Holy Spirit is creating among us.

[5] Church planting is part of the Church Development characteristic that Nazarenes practice globally. For a fuller explanation, see "Our Nazarene Characteristics 1.1." This can be found on the web at www.nazarene.org/essentials.

[6] *Nazarene Manual*, 2017 – 2021, par 11, p 33.

[7] A spirit of repentance is vital for believers to experience "the continued perfecting work of the Holy Spirit." This spirit is crucial for the development of "a mature character" and "growth in grace." It is the primary attitude believers are to "give careful attention to" in the "process of spiritual development and improvement of Christlike character and personality" (Nazarene Manual, Article of Faith X, Christian Holi-

ness and Entire Sanctification). We encourage superintendents, pastors, professors, etc. to model and teach the importance of a spirit of repentance in the lives of every member, in every local church and in every classroom.

[8] This is how John Wesley describes the doctrine of entire sanctification or Christian perfection – "purity of intention, dedicating all the life to God." For a numbered list of Wesley's steps toward understanding what he termed "perfect love," we encourage everyone to read his famous sermon, "A Plain Account of Christian Perfection."

Chapter 5

[1] This New Testament practice of interdependence is also the way Nazarene districts operate today. Every Nazarene district throughout the world is designed "to be an entity of interdependent local churches" (Nazarene Manual, par 200).

[2] For a description of the local, district and global church, see "The Church 1.1," a document that can be found on the web at www.nazarene.org/essentials.

[3] There is strong biblical support in James for John Wesley's teaching, "there is no holiness without social holiness." As church members, we cannot live holy lives in isolation. At least one other person needs to know everything about our spiritual journey and hold us accountable before God for "improvement in Christlikeness of character" (Nazarene Manual, par 10). Without this honest accountability, as was present in early Methodism's classes and bands, the practice of "confessing your sins to each other and praying for each other that you may be healed" (James 5:16), is absent in the church. We encourage EVERY Nazarene to find an accountability partner for help in living an accountable, holy life.

[4] The General Assembly is the "supreme doctrine-formulating, law-making, and elective authority of the Church of the Nazarene" (*Nazarene Manual*, par 300).

[5] "Market cap" is a term that refers to the market capitalization or value of a company's outstanding shares of stock. When a person buys "shares," they become part owner in the company.

[6] GDP (Gross Domestic Product) is the total value of the goods produced and services provided in a country during one year.

[7] The World Bank is an international organization dedicated to providing financing, advice and research to developing nations. It attempts to fight poverty by offering development assistance to middle and low-income countries.

Chapter 6

[1] This is a quote from "Our Wesleyan Holiness Heritage 1.2." This document can be found on the web at www.nazarene.org/essentials.

[2] For the biblical references to martyrs, see Matthew 10:21-22; Acts 7:58, 12:2, 21:13; Hebrews 11:37; Revelation 2:10,13, 6:9 and 20:4.

[3] In the year 2000, while planting two new churches out of Grand Rapids First Church, Pastor Joe Knight introduced the concept of "corporate sanctification" to the church. While the idea has been nurtured and taught by others in recent years, we find the theological roots of this principle in the teachings of Jesus.

[4] We believe it is possible for a church at the end of its life-cycle to close and choose to be a multiplying church! As Nazarenes, we see the movement of God through the people of God as more important than one local church. We will explain more about the church life-cycle in Book 2 of the **MULTIPLYNAZ** series.

[5] The biblical basis for churches making missional multiplication decisions can be found in 2 Chronicles 15:7; Psalm 51:17; Jeremiah 24:7; John 9:4, 12:24, 17:17-23 and Luke 6:38.

[6] A mina was about three months' wages. In this parable of Jesus, the servants were given a considerable amount of money to invest and a return on this investment was expected.

[7] The insights here are found in the *Life Application Bible* (Luke 19:11-27), Tyndale House and Zondervan, 1991.

[8] A study of the harmony of the Gospels supports the idea that there were more than 25 events Jesus experienced in the first 6-9 months of ministry with his disciples before he spent all night in prayer and selected the Twelve (Luke 6:12-13).

[9] Article VII in our Articles of Faith explain how God's prevenient grace draws people to faith. These articles with supporting Scriptures listed can be found in can be found in "Our Articles of Faith 1.1," located on the web at www.nazarene.org/essentials.

[10] How Nazarenes recognize the strengths and equality of churches and leaders from all countries is more fully explained in "Our Global Church 1.2." This document can be found on the web at www.nazarene.org/essentials.

Chapter 7

[1] Special thanks go to a Leadership Network article in their July 2015 newsletter that stimulated this paragraph.

[2] We are grateful to both Lonnie Bullock and Phil Stevenson for their contribution to the development of "the three circles" concept several years ago when they worked with Larry McKain as consultants at New Church Specialties.

[3] We first heard this principle taught by Dan Croy, a professor from Point Loma Nazarene University. Our movement enjoys an incredible team of professors in 51 institutions of learning who impact the future of the church every day in their classrooms.

[4] A biblical example of shared vision is the Philippi church planting team led by Paul (Acts 16:10). Paul received the vision, but it did not remain "his vision." The Scriptures declare, "After Paul had seen the vision, **we** got ready at once to leave for Macedonia, concluding that God had called **us** to preach the gospel to them." At this point, the vision was no longer just an individual vision—it became a "shared vision" by the whole team.

[5] In Book Two of the **MULTIPLYNAZ** series, we will discuss in greater detail how the spiritual planning a church does is guided by developing a shared vision.

[6] Scripture abounds with examples of how trust is foundational to effective leadership. Some examples include Exodus 14:31, 18:21; Proverbs 11:13, 12:22, 13:17, 25:13, 27:6; Luke 16:10; 1 Corinthians 4:2, 13:7 and 1 Timothy 1:12.

[7] Patrick Lencioni, *Five Dysfunctions of a Team: A Leadership Fable* (San Francisco, CA, Jossey-Bass, 2002).

[8] This has been a foundational statement for the Church of the Nazarene since our beginnings. It is found in the forward of the Nazarene Manual.

[9] We are thankful for these spiritual insights on prayer from Pastor Corey Jones, of Crossroads Tabernacle in Dallas, Texas.

[10] In the future we will explore how God's passion (spiritual enthusiasm), can powerfully work in a believer's life. Enthusiasm comes from the Greek word "in theos" meaning being "in God." Spending time with Jesus, remaining in him, having his Word remain in us and bringing the Father glory cause fruitfulness and show that we are Christlike disciples (John 15:5-8).

CPSIA information can be obtained
at www.ICGtesting.com
Printed in the USA
FSHW011355280521
81773FS